THE PRACTICAL QABALAH

THE PRACTICAL QABALAH

Charles Fielding

SAMUEL WEISER, INC.

York Beach, Maine

First published in 1989 by
Samuel Weiser, Inc.
Box 612
York Beach, Maine 03910

01 00 99 98 97 96 95
10 9 8 7 6 5 4 3 2

Library of Congress Cataloging-in-Publication Data
Fielding, Charles
     The practical qabalah / by Charles Fielding.
        p. cm.
     1. Cabala. 2. Occultism. I. Title
BF1611.F45   1989
135' .4—dc20
ISBN 0-87728-654-X   89-9188
                                                               CIP

Typeset in 11 point Goudy
Printed in the United States of America

Contents

Acknowledgment

Some of the material in this book has been based on the work of Dion Fortune and the group she founded, the Society of the Inner Light. The author gratefully acknowledges the help and inspiration provided by these sources.

Preface

When I first got interested in the occult, quite a long time ago, my first impulse was to read as many books as possible. This was not too difficult; there were plenty of books and I read and re-read them avidly until they came out of my ears. I thought about occultism and dreamt about occultism, and probably became a fine example of a narrow-minded bigot.

After a while, common sense and disillusionment restored a degree of sanity. I was still enthusiastic and excited. I still felt that I was on a quest, like the knights of old. But, like Arthur's far from perfect followers, I was slowly and painfully gaining wisdom—not a lot, but it was a start.

In the course of my occult education I discovered that there were very few useful books; most were only fit for burning. There were some brilliant exceptions. Notable among these were the books of Dion Fortune; *The Mystical Qabalah, The Training and Work of an Initiate, Sane Occultism, The Esoteric Orders and Their Work,* and the abstract and metaphysical *Cosmic Doctrine.*[1] I was rather young and very ignorant, but it seemed to me that here was an author who knew her subject from first-hand experience, not hearsay, and her writing became a valued source of information.

There were other books, too; books that were spoken of with bated breath, not just because they were long out of print and sold at inflated prices, but because they were believed to contain "the occult secrets." These awesome tomes included the four volumes of *The Golden Dawn*[2] and the works of Aleister Crowley.

---

[1]These titles are still available from Aquarian Press, Wellingborough, England, and Samuel Weiser, York Beach, ME.
[2]*The Golden Dawn* (Chicago: Aries Press, 1936–1940).

The latter gained an added savour from this author's notoriety; for by Crowley's own proclamation he was "the wickedest man in the world!" I lusted after these forbidden fruits.

As time went on, more and more of these special books were re-published and became freely available. And it soon became apparent that in all the mass of material, there was much that was interesting and some that was useful—but no "secrets."

The truth is that the great secrets of occultism are gained by experience, not by reading. A "Mystery" is defined as "a truth which is beyond reason," so it can hardly be written down in a book. To find the Holy Grail we have to make a journey; and we cannot ride an armchair!

Dion Fortune's books appeal because their attitude is practical. In reading them, we share an experience, rather than merely gaining knowledge. But despite their great value, her works are now more than half a century old, and the Golden Dawn material nearer the century.

Times have changed and so have attitudes. Much that was previously "occult" is now common knowledge and information that was once confined to the Lodge can now be discussed.

The purpose of this book and its companion volumes is to publish as much of the Western Esoteric Tradition as can be put to good use in the modern world and to indicate one way whereby the personal quest for the Grail can be attempted. The Qabalah is one such way; it is an eminently practical system for the modern Westerner.

Some people are natural "solitaries," while others prefer to work in organized groups. I hope this book and those that follow will be useful to both approaches. Finally, it is said that books speak to the unconscious and lift thought to the same source as originally inspired them. I hope that this book fulfills these requirements.

May your quest be as exciting an adventure as mine has been.

CHAPTER ONE

Foundations of Western Occultism

THIS IS A book about occultism. It is written for average, intelligent people who are interested enough to find out more about it. The word "occult" means "hidden"—just that; but the subject has been so misunderstood and distorted by late night movies, superstition and a sensational press, that it is often condemned as spectacular garbage. Men and women of all races have studied this subject since earliest history and rumor says that many of the world's most eminent people have made it their life study and owe their greatness to its practice.

Study of the Qabalah and its great symbol, The Tree of Life, is probably one of the best ways of introducing yourself to occult theory and practice. To do justice to qabalistic theories and methods, it is important to see them against a realistic background. What do modern qabalists think? Why are they devoting time and attention to a subject already ancient when Jesus was born? What are they trying to achieve?

These are all very reasonable questions. So, before we start looking at the Qabalah itself, we ought to examine the basic ideas of modern occultism in the Western world. Not every occultist would subscribe to all the ideas put forward here. As in modern science, there are differences in interpretation and disagreements about details. What follows is a reasonable synopsis of current occult thinking.

Once upon a time, as the story books say, all knowledge of mankind and the world we live in was studied under the discipline of philosophy, which means "love of wisdom." Physics and psychology rubbed shoulders with chemistry, metaphysics and ethics, because all of these subjects were believed to be parts of one great system.

As time went on, certain subjects—notably physics and chemistry—developed away from their philosophic parent and developed the arrogant independence of the adolescent. Even psychology renounced its origins and declared a unilateral independence.

From all this growth was Western technological civilization born and many of our social habits and morals derived. Despite its detractors, Western science is a remarkable tribute to human creativity. But we are beginning to realize that our civilization is a very unbalanced system and that some central concept of purpose and unity must be sought if civilization is not to destroy itself.

The great civilizations of the East have not succeeded any better. The West has produced an environment technologically advanced, but emotionally and spiritually arid, while the East's great philosophical and psycho-spiritual growth now withers in surroundings of poverty, ignorance and squalor. Something must surely be wrong somewhere.

But there are gleams of light dawning in the darkness. Modern science is showing signs of approaching adulthood. The universe of Einstein and the particle physicists is a far cry from the mindless mechanisms of Victorian science. Physics is fast becoming a life-science, and the divisions between mind and matter are being eroded slowly but surely. So what of occultism from all this?

Properly understood, occultism is the study of mind and matter, God and humanity, origins and destiny. It is the true Science of Life.

What then are the basics of occult belief? The first thing to understand is that occultism has no creed: there is no "I believe. . . ." Instead, like science, there are a number of hypotheses. Now a hypothesis is an idea which seems to work when put into practice but which can be modified in the light of further experience. Occultism is the Science of Life. Life evolves and with it, experience. So having made it clear that there are no occult dogmas, let us examine some of these basic ideas, and see how they appeal to us.

First, occultists think that there is an invisible reality behind what we see and experience in the physical world and that this reality is the hidden cause behind all the appearances of the world about us. This seems reasonable enough when you consider that science says much the same thing. After all, gravity is, in one sense, an "invisible reality." You can't see it, but it works. The only difference here between scientists and occultists is that the latter extend the hypothesis beyond the tangible world.

The next hypothesis concerns purpose: "What is the meaning of it all?" At one time, many scientists considered the universe a cosmic accident and life a biochemical fluke. Recently, some of them seem to be changing their minds.

Occultists consider that nothing is without a purpose. They reason that there must be a supreme plan for the creation and evolution of the universe which embraces galaxies and solar systems, suns and planets, atoms, plants, animals, *and* humanity. Within this supreme plan are the countless lesser plans of all creation, each of them interlocked and interrelated into one organic whole. They suggest that we—as an intelligent life-form having the power of choice—have a vital task to play in the continuous unfolding of the supreme plan.

As to what vast mechanism might contain and administer that plan, you must make your own choice. If religious, then you can conceive of God as the origin and prime-mover. If agnostic, you might prefer to imagine some vast cosmic "system." After all, we are only using words and it is the idea that matters.

Following on from the plan comes the idea of universal evolution in which we move from a simple and uncoordinated state to a wonderful condition of harmonious and highly developed perfection, each element of the plan having developed its own lesser plan to the highest excellence that its structure allows.

Now we, in our essential nature, are considered as nuclei of intelligent energy. As such we are self-motivating creators in our own right, eternal and indestructible. One of the cornerstones of occult thinking is the proposal that the human does not have to live through a physical body and that our involvement with matter is simply one of many phases through which we pass in our evolution. Nevertheless, working through a body is considered to be a vital aspect of our education because it teaches us control of dense matter—a condition far removed from our natural condition of freedom.

Now this introduces the idea of reincarnation. Reincarnation is the notion that we get through many bodies in the process of learning about the dense matter of the physical world. One short span of seventy or eighty years is no way sufficient to learn all the lessons and put right all the mistakes. The idea of reincarnation is a great liberator. Instead of one life, win or lose— the concept of reincarnation gives us a chance to learn from mistakes and move forward with the excitement of new challenges to meet, and the prospect of fresh conquests.

When the idea of reincarnation is accepted as a working fact and when it is realized that there is always more living to come and new opportunities to explore, then where is the sting of death? Occultists have always maintained that our first major victory lies in conquering this fear. In this lies the first great freedom.

Occultists lay great stress upon the matter of personal responsibility. If the idea of continuing evolution is accepted, then race and circumstances are no mere accidents of birth. Nationality, state of health, amount of money, and personality characteristics in each new life are the result of past successes and failures.

The circumstances of life at any moment in time offer the perfect environment for the next lesson in physical experience. And, if this idea is taken on trust, then it follows that we are totally responsible for the circumstances in which we find our-selves, no matter how hard this may seem to us.

"As a man sows, so also shall he reap," "Cast your bread upon the waters. . . ," and so on, are all statements based upon this idea. In the philosophy of the East it is called karma, the law of cause and effect. There are no straight lines in the universe. Every thought or action returns eventually to its point of origin—like a boomerang.

Ultimately, the inner person completes its term in physical matter having learned all its lessons. But evolution goes on and physical experience is only a small part of it. What happens, then, to one who is "free of the wheel of birth and death"? Well, we have free will, so we can choose. It is said that there are two basic choices: either to go on or to remain.

Some may choose to continue their experience on non-physical levels, moving away from their fellow students who are still in the classroom of matter. Others may decide to remain near the physical world to help. Occultists call these helpers of humanity "Inner Plane Adepts," and believe they have chosen to guide and instruct less-evolved companions on Earth.

This must surely raise another question. How can a being without a body "guide and instruct" one who is still in the flesh? How can communication be established? Well, if one can accept that there is more to us than just the body, then it follows that a part of us must be non-physical. If that is so, then it is reasonable to suppose that the non-physical part is capable of functioning in the invisible world that lies behind physical matter, just as the material body functions in the ordinary world. So the idea is that the Inner Plane Adept talks to our non-physical part and the communication is passed to the brain and becomes a conscious thought. Basically it can be thought of as telepathy between a discarnate and an incarnate being.

These are the foundations of the Western occult system of thought. Some concepts I have mentioned may be accepted immediately as true, others might rate as "non-proven." If what occultism says is true then it doesn't matter, because when you follow the system, you will ultimately find out for yourself. Direct experience is the only way.

Now you can do one of three things. You can throw this book away in disgust. You can read on for intellectual stimulation. Or you can read on determined to gain enough knowledge to put these ideas to the test. You have free will—the choice is yours.

CHAPTER TWO

An Introduction to the Qabalah

YOU ARE SEEKING the invisible reality. All readers of this book are searching, in some way or other, for that invisible reality we discussed in the last chapter. That is what this book is all about. But there are difficulties. It is not easy to use everyday language to discuss things that are supposed to be real, yet somehow invisible! Sometimes words are useless.

The Western Occult Tradition aims to bring invisible reality down to earth, to ground it and (eventually!) bring about the kingdom on earth. To accomplish this formidable task, we need to be able to come to grips with ideas that are, in the everyday world, unthinkable.

Signs, Symbols and Glyphs

Consider for a moment your ordinary thoughts and ideas. Everyday thoughts are most often expressed in words. In fact, in many people, a thought may become conscious as "words in the head." A thought like "I need a haircut" often appears as mental words. Other thoughts may come into the mind as a mixture of words and pictures. Emotionally colored thoughts often bring a picture with them. Most of our thinking in Western society is a wordy operation.

Ideas are rather different. It is true that "mental" rather than "emotional" people frequently clothe ideas in words; but often ideas are more pictorial and are associated with feeling. Sometimes words can be long-winded and clumsy and we often use *signs* to signify common ideas. One obvious example is road signs, where a simple design, an "ideogram," can replace words to good advantage. In this book we shall be using the word "sign" in the same way as many psychologists might—meaning *a substitution for the real thing or a representation of it.* Other examples of signs are a "food" emblem consisting of a knife and fork enclosed in a circle and a lighted cigarette enclosed in a circle with a bar across it, meaning that smoking is forbidden. There are, of course, many more, such as the internationally agreed sign for radioactivity.

Sometimes *compound signs* are used—a group of signs arranged to show a set of relationships or the flow of data within some system. The circuit diagrams of electronics and the flowcharts used by computer programmers are examples. Signs, whether single or compound, are shorthand that represents

Figure 1. The road sign for food (A) is one that you recognize no matter what language you speak. Occult signs and symbols (B, the Christian Cross) speak to you in the same way.

thoughts or objects or processes as shown in figure 1a. There is no feeling in them.

Let us get back to words. Words are signs because they represent thoughts and things. Quite complex ideas can be depicted by words. But words can also be used to tune the mood of the reader by painting mental pictures, though even in expert hands they are often quite inadequate. Poets are masters at using words to describe an image of something, but it is the *image* that represents the significance of the thing with its attendant emotions and feelings. The more brilliant the poet, the more effective the word-image. But there is still a limit to what can be achieved by words alone.

We will consider *images*—the pictures left in the mind when the words of the poet have faded away. The sort of image we are describing is not a sign; it is not merely a convenient shorthand for something ordinary. Rather is it a *symbol,* an ideogram depicting some state or process which cannot adequately be put into words. In fact that gives us our definition for a symbol—*an image that depicts something that could not otherwise adequately be described.* Signs are essentially mental things. Symbols are involved with feelings on some level or other. Signs are surface products of the recently acquired logical mind; symbols, on the other hand, evoke the depths, the great and fundamental simplicities on which humanity is based. Signs are conscious; symbols belong to the unconscious. The way to superconsciousness is through the unconscious, therefore symbols are the tools of the occultist.

Try making a mental picture of the Christian cross (see figure 1b). Even to an atheist it evokes the whole concept of Christianity, in particular the sacrificial death of its founder. To the devout Christian, its associations are practically limitless— from the mystical idea of vicarious sacrifice to the higher emotions of devotion, idealism, piety, and so on. Of course, to the atheist the cross may also evoke strong feelings of irritation and annoyance at the apparent futility of it all! But one thing is certain— *feelings* will be aroused. Everyone is likely to react emotionally in some way to some degree.

Symbols have degrees of profundity and universality. Human beings are very different and a given symbol may mean much to one and little to another in the same way that music and pictures enthrall one and bore another. The more archetypal a symbol, the more universal its power and appeal. Symbols may depict aspects of the soul or the universe; the "inside" or the "outside." If modern physicists had their say, they would probably declare inside and outside to be the same thing from different angles.

Occultists use symbols extensively to depict the incomprehensible, to comprehend the inconceivable, and to control the unimaginable. We are tool-using creatures and employ symbols as tools so we can understand the nature of the invisible reality and work with it, both within ourselves and within the soul of nature. Most of the symbols used in Western occultism are archetypal. Many are very old; some go back to the earliest time of our organization on this planet.

If the human is considered in a fourfold way as spirit, mind, emotions and body, then there are grades of symbols suitable for each level. The simplest, most abstract symbols are *geometrical*: the point, line, circle, polygon, and so on. The next level, sometimes called *compound symbols,* include such images as the cross, ankh, star of David, and pentacle. The third level, characterized by its human or animal imagery, may be called *personalized.* Ezekiel's "Four Holy Living Creatures"—the man, lion, eagle and bull—come into this category as do the anthropoid forms of archangel, Mary the mother of God, Jesus as crucified savior, and Christ the king. You can probably think of many more. The fourth level is not made up of single symbols, but of specially selected imagery linked together like a chain. In practice, this *dynamic symbol set* is arranged like a visual journey within which we "move" from one state of consciousness to another. These inner journeys are called *pathworkings* by the modern qabalist; we shall be dealing with them later in some detail.

If you look at the four levels of symbols we have described, you will see that they represent increasing levels of complexity, as do the four levels of mankind. You will realize that *geometrical* symbols apply to the most abstract level—the spirit or the first cause in the universe. A point has position but no dimension. A line is an extended point, a point thrusting out toward infinity. A circle is a line which returns to the point from which it started, a sort of endless track making an enclosure in which "space" is confined. Polygons—squares, triangles, hexagons and so on—represent special types of enclosures whose significance is determined by the number of their sides.

The *compound* symbols depict more complex ideas, as you would expect. For example, the pentacle (or five-pointed star) depicts the special relationship between the four alchemical elements (earth, air, fire and water) and the fifth condition—aether—from which they originated. The pentacle represents our four levels and their relationship with spirit. This symbol is often used in ceremonial occultism. Another form of star is the hexagram, this time six-pointed. It is made up of two interlaced triangles, one pointing up and the other down. The first represents matter aspiring "upwards" to spirit; the second, the spiritual principles driving "downward" into matter. As a whole, this symbol depicts perfection—in the first case, God-in-Man, in the second, the kingdom on earth. As you will see, compound symbols belong to the level of mind.

Personalized symbols—the third level—apply mostly to our emotional or feeling parts, or to the equivalent levels of energy in the universe. You can recognize them by their human or animal form. Whereas the first two types of symbols represented principles and ideas respectively, this third category depicts experience which is essentially *human*, normally encountered as feelings and emotions. In this case the heart is speaking rather than the head. Consider for a moment the delectable Greek goddess Aphrodite, every young man's dream girl, or the hunky hero Heracles, fresh from his latest good-guy episode. Think (or rather feel) about the glorious Titan Helios driving the chariot of the sun across the azure sky, or about the blue-robed Mary, mother of Jesus, or about the Egyptian Horus, Hawk of the Morning.

Surely, one or more of these images evoke feelings of one sort or another? They are all typical of this class of symbols.

I think we have said enough about symbols to make it clear that they appeal to the inner self—to spirit, higher mind and emotions—in a way that words could never do. Symbols represent the eternal verities. These ancient truths are realities in the soul, often pushed underground in modern Westerners who have forgotten where they came from, where they are going, and who their parents are.

When discussing signs, we mentioned compound signs— diagrams depicting flows, processes, and relationships. In the same way, symbols can be grouped together to form *compound symbols*, sometimes called *glyphs*. Glyphs can take various forms and have many uses. Glyphs comprise whole alphabets of images and can be thought of as super-symbols.

Of all the glyphs used in Western occultism, the supreme example is the Tree of Life of the Qabalah, called in Hebrew *Otz Chiim*. This diagram of ten circles and twenty-two interconnecting lines supports a whole library of symbols, from the simple geometrical to complex personalized forms. This glyph is the basis of magical ritual and pathworking. It is the key to the occult philosophy, anatomy, and physiology of the West. It is *the* great glyph of the soul of humanity and of nature. The symbolism contained in the Tree of Life will repay a lifetime of study.

Qabalistic Symbols

The Tree of Life is the foundation glyph of the Western Occult Tradition and has been used for meditation and practical occult work for countless years. Many of its symbols are archetypal, which means that they have deep meaning for people of all races and creeds. They embody fundamental human experiences like "maleness," "femaleness," "motherhood," and so on. Centuries of occult students who have been raised on this symbolism and trained in its practical use, begin to live, move and think within this system. We work with it daily, meditating upon it and interpreting life in the light of its structure. It brings order to the inner life; dreams and "psychism" will appear in terms of the Tree's symbolism and, when we reach the appropriate stage of training, ritual work will be based upon it.

For the Qabalah to become a part of our lives, its use must be quite automatic if we are to gain the full benefit. For this reason, it is a good idea to make notes and draw diagrams at every opportunity. In this way, the system becomes a part of our inner world.

We shall be concentrating on the Qabalah and its Tree of Life for the next few chapters, so we ought to spend a little time thinking about the origins of this great system. The word *Qabalah* (Kabbalah or Cabbala) comes from the Hebrew *QBL, Cabal*, which means *to receive*. So the Qabalah is "that which has been received." As to where it first originated, the ancient rabbis would have said that it was given to us by the angels. There was certainly some secrecy surrounding its past, which may be responsible for the fact that, while most scholars place its origins in the Middle Ages, occult tradition maintains that the Qabalah is prehistoric. Qabalistic writings certainly appeared in medieval times, but an oral tradition probably existed long before that time, passed on "from mouth to ear" by generations of teachers to their students. Some authorities have considered that resemblances between the Zoroastrian *Zend Avesta* and the Qabalah indicate that Jews may have received the basics of the system from the same source as Zoroaster. After all, during the exile, Daniel was known as Beltheshazzar, the Great Magician of Babylon.

Most modern students are not overly interested in academic research for its own sake; they want something they can use now. The Qabalah is a living system and grows with use. It has evolved, as must all systems of knowledge if they are to survive. The Qabalistic material is often classified under four headings:

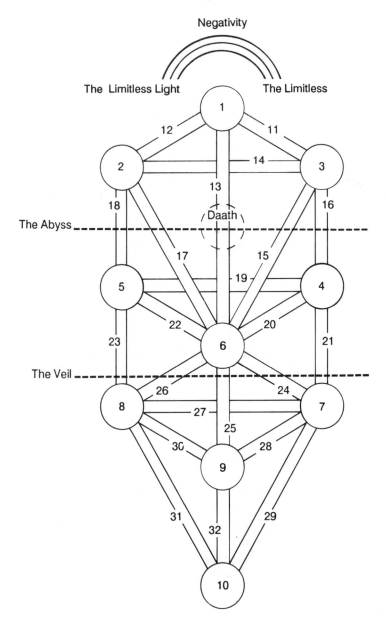

Figure 2. The Tree of Life.

1) Practical Qabalah, which deals with ceremonial magic;

2) Dogmatic Qabalah, which comprises the literature of the system;

3) Literal Qabalah, which deals with letters and their numeric values;

4) Unwritten Qabalah, which is concerned with the attribution of symbols to the spheres of the Tree of Life.

Of these four divisions, the practicing Western occultist is mostly concerned with the practical and unwritten Qabalah, although some work is still done with numerology involving Hebrew letters and words, which forms part of the literal Qabalah.

The Triangles on the Tree

Otz Chiim, the Tree of Life, is truly the Tree of the Knowledge of Good and Evil. It is made up of ten circles or spheres called *sephiroth,* meaning "emanations." The singular form of *sephiroth* is *sephirah.* These sephiroth are arranged in three triangles with the tenth alone at the bottom, as shown in figure 2 on page 14.

The triangles on the Tree are interconnected by twenty-two lines or *paths,* but we shall ignore the paths for the moment. Study figure 3a on page 16 and get its general shape clear in your mind. The circles in figure 2 represent stages in the development of things—in particular the development of the universe and the soul. The circles are numbered from 1 to 10 in accordance with a zigzag line called *the lightning flash,* which is sometimes attached to the diagram of the Tree. See figure 3b on page 16.

In case you are wondering why the spheres on the Tree cannot just be strung out in a line like a row of beads, the answer is that the Tree represents a set of relationships, not merely a sequence of events.

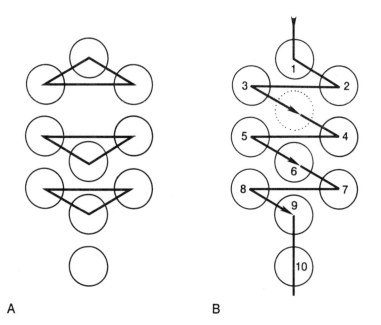

A   B

Figure 3. The Triangles on the Tree are shown in (A), while in (B) we see the Lightning Flash.

The Pillars

The ten spheres on the Tree can be considered as three vertical lines or *pillars*. This arrangement shows the three great complementary principles of activity, passivity, and equilibrium. The side pillars always represent the complementaries, while the middle pillar depicts the state of balance between them. See figure 4.

Pillar symbolism, like all relationships on the Tree, can be applied equally to humanity or to the universe. The significance of complementary forces on the Tree will become clearer as we continue our investigation. You will notice a dotted circle between circles one and six; this represents an "invisible sephirah" called *Daath* which we shall talk about later. In Qabalistic tradi-

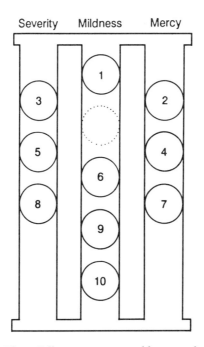

Figure 4. The Three Pillars: severity, mildness and mercy.

tion, the pillars were often called *Severity* (active), *Mercy* (passive) and *Mildness* (equilibrium).

The Hebrew Letters

A professor of Hebrew at an English university is said to have started his first lecture with the words, "Ladies and Gentlemen, this is the language which God spoke." Perhaps he was being a little exclusive, but he had a good point to make. Certainly, a substantial part of the sacred scriptures of the Western culture was first recorded in this ancient language.

There are twenty-two letters in the Hebrew alphabet. All are consonants. The vowel sounds, or "points," were added later. Legend said that during the Creation God paraded the twenty-two letters before Him and "saw that they were good." Having received divine approval, the letters were considered holy, each representing a concept and a sound. The actual shape of the letters is similar to the objects which they were originally supposed to represent. Thus *Shin,* the twenty-first letter, represents a serpent's fang; while *Kaph,* the eleventh, depicts a palm.

Hebrew has always fascinated gentile occultists because it is old and looks strange and mysterious. Its sounds are unusual and sometimes gutteral, and suggest curious and secret things outside the bounds of ordinary human life. At this point you may be wondering whether you will be required to learn Hebrew before understanding the Tree and using it. The answer is a simple "no." The Tree is a system of relationships which is universal. It can be expressed in any language and in any age.

Since the Tree can be used effectively with no knowledge of Hebrew, why then are we digressing to consider this language? First, because the Qabalistic ideas were first expressed in Hebrew and a great deal of subsequent writing, such as the Golden Dawn material, based much of its theory and practice upon the letters and their meanings. And, secondly, because centuries of occult students meditating and working upon them in ritual have made Hebrew a kind of focus in the unconscious of the Western Occult Tradition. The modern occultist, so the theory says, by meditation on the letters, can tune in to this pool of ideas and experience. You must try this for yourself. Some find it helpful; others do not. Nevertheless, if you want to study the literature of the Qabalah and the Tree of Life, a basic knowledge of how the letters apply to the Tree is necessary. So we shall introduce them as our discussion continues.

As we said, there are twenty-two letters, all consonants. Hebrew has no separate signs for numbers, so each letter is given a numeric value. The ancient rabbis used this peculiarity in developing a form of numerology called *gematria.* If the values of the separate letters making up a word are totalled, the sum obtained can be compared with the results applied to other words. All words having a common total are considered to have a special affinity. The letters themselves are used on the Tree in a way we shall discuss later, so although you are not obliged to use them, they are worth getting to know.

Qabalists divide the letters into three groups: the *mother letters*, the *double letters* and the *single letters*. There are three mother, seven double and twelve single letters. But more later. Table 1 on page 20 provides a summary.

This digression away from our basic explanation of the structure of the Tree has been necessary because the letters and their numerical values will appear from now on as we continue.

The Tree as a Whole

So far we have been looking at the Tree as if it were simply ten circles arranged in a pattern. These circles fall into three triangles plus one circle at the bottom. They can also be considered as three vertical pillars. There are other important patterns, too, but they will not mean very much until we have looked at the Tree as a whole.

Looking back at figure 2 (on page 14) you will see the ten sephiroth joined together by the twenty-two lines or paths. Each sphere is numbered as shown in the Lightning Flash (figure 3b on page 16) and also bears a Hebrew name. The paths are numbered, starting with 11 (continuing the number sequence of the sephiroth), and finishing at 32 at the bottom of the glyph. The whole diagram makes up the "32 Marvellous Tracts of Wisdom." The letters are attached to the paths, not the sephiroth. Aleph, the first, is assigned to the first path, number 11. Tau, the last, is placed upon the final path, the 32nd.

Have a look at the diagram of the Tree and get straight on the numbering. If you draw your own Tree and make a few copies of it, you can add other symbols as we discuss them. For example, you could practice writing the Hebrew letters and copy them in alongside the paths.

Table 1. The Hebrew Letters

Letter	Pronunciation	Representation	Value	Type
א	Aleph	Ox	1	Mother
ב	Beth	House	2	Double
ג	Gimel	Camel	3	Double
ד	Daleth	Door	4	Double
ה	He	Window	5	Single
ו	Vau	Nail	6	Single
ז	Zain	Sword	7	Single
ח	Cheth	Fence	8	Single
ט	Teth	Serpent	9	Single
י	Yod	Hand	10	Single
כך	Kaph	Palm	20 (500)	Double
ל	Lamed	Ox Goad	30	Single
מם	Mem	Water	40 (600)	Mother
נן	Nun	Fish	50 (700)	Single
ס	Samekh	Prop	60	Single
ע	Ayin	Eye	70	Single
פף	Pe	Mouth	80 (800)	Double
צץ	Tzaddi	Fishhook	90 (900)	Single

Table 1. The Hebrew Letters (*continued*)

Letter	Pronunciation	Representation	Value	Type
ק	Qoph	Back of Head	100	Single
ר	Resh	Head	200	Double
שׁ	Shin	Tooth	300	Mother
ת	Tau	Tau Cross	400	Double

Now for an important idea. The Tree is a *relative* symbol, not an absolute one. The glyph represents ten basic states and the *relationships* between them. The first sephirah always represents the starting point of something—the first state, the prime-mover, the origin. The last sephirah, Malkuth, depicts the final condition—the outcome, the end of the matter. The other sephiroth indicate stages between beginning and ending, and the relationship between the stages.

In using the Tree, we choose one of the sephiroth, usually the first or the last, and associate it with some concept we are trying to understand. We then use the rest of the glyph to depict associated conditions. For example, suppose we are looking for understanding of the inner nature of mankind. We could associate the first sephirah with the highest aspect of humanity, the prime-mover, spirit. The tenth sephirah could then be used to represent the end-result, the densest and most complex manifestation of Spirit—the physical body. The intermediate sephiroth would then symbolize mind, emotions and instincts, the conditions "between" the first state and the last.

Or, to take another example: consider Kether, the 1st sephirah, as the first cause or God. Then the last sphere, Malkuth, could depict God's creation, the universe. The intermediate sephiroth could then be considered as the stages and inter-relationships of evolution.

An idea can be associated with an intermediate sphere. Still thinking of the universe, our own sun—with all its religious and mythological associations—could be "attached" to the 6th sephirah, Tiphareth. Planet earth could then be assigned to Malkuth; leaving the first sephirah, Kether, to symbolize the first cause (whatever you consider that to be).

We will need more data for detailed examples. However, we now know that the glyph is certainly not a rigid set of symbols whose meanings are fixed for all time. Instead we have a philosophical, psychological, and magical instrument of great versatility. Like any other tool, we have to learn to use it.

The paths have still not been considered in detail. For the moment it is enough to consider the sephiroth as depicting forces, concepts or conditions; while the paths represent stages of change between one sephirotic condition and another.

The Sephiroth

Each of the ten sephiroth is given a title. See Table 2 for the definitions and common pronunciations. Some of these names are full of meaning and give many clues as to the significance of the sphere. For instance, Kether, the title of the first sephirah, means "the Crown." Crowns are associated with kings and queens; crowns rest on top of the head; they are higher than the head itself; and so we could continue. It is worth spending a few moments now and then letting your mind play gently around the ideas suggested by the titles. At any rate, Malkuth, Netzach and Hod should make you think with their titles of *the kingdom, the power,* and *the glory.* In order to get accustomed to the sephirotic titles, we shall be using them instead of numbers for a while.

Remember, the way to learn about the Tree is to use it. Draw the glyph often, make notes about it, speculate about it and cogitate upon its symbols. Let us now use it as a diagram representing the process of the descent of the universe into matter, from its origin to its material form. The sequence follows the path taken by the Lightning Flash. (See figure 3b on page 16.)

Table 2. Sephirotic Titles

Sephirah	Title	Pronunciation	Definition
1	Kether	Ké-ther	The Crown
2	Chokmah	Hok-mah (h as in hot)	Wisdom
3	Binah	Bee-nah	Understanding
4	Chesed	Hess-ed	Mercy (or Majesty)
5	Geburah	Gebb-u-rah	Severity (or strength)
6	Tiphareth	Tiph-a-reth	Beauty (or Equilibrium)
7	Netzach	Nett-zach (ch as in loch)	Victory (or Power)
8	Hod	Hod (o as in load)	Glory
9	Yesod	Yess-od (o as in load)	The Foundation
10	Malkuth	Mal-kuth	The Kingdom

Now look at figure 5 on page 24. First find Kether on the Tree. You will see three bands of radiance above it. These are called *the three veils*. The idea is that Kether must have come from somewhere, and the veils represent the previous condition from which Kether emerged. The outermost veil is called *negativity*, the next, *the limitless*, and the one nearest to Kether, *the limitless light*. These ideas are discussed in the section in Cosmogony.

Out of the limitless light crystallized the primal point, Kether. Perfect and self-sustaining, it remains in eternity, the focus of a circle whose center is everywhere and whose circumference is nowhere. Then, obeying some mystery of its nature, or a

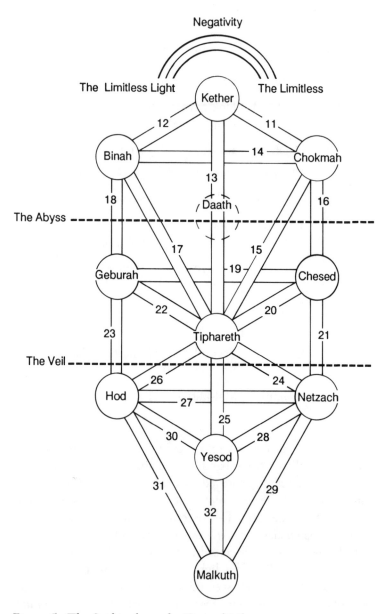

Figure 5. The Sephiroth on the Tree of Life.

call from the limitless ocean of negative light which gave it birth, it generated motion. With a roar of silence, the limitless energy of Kether broke bounds and escaped into the infinite void. This incredible movement of pure existence can be symbolized by Chokmah.

But action generates reaction in any closed system; and this system, almost infinite in its magnitude, is yet bounded by the sphere of attention of its creator. There are no straight lines in the cosmos. Reactive forces make the straight line into a curve and, ultimately, a circle. The boundless thrusting energy of Chokmah has been confined, locked in a circle of its own making. As unconditioned force it has died; but in dying has given birth to the first idea of form, a closed circle of energy, symbolized on the Tree by the third sephirah, Binah.

These first three sephiroth form a pattern of great significance, a triangle which is repeated at lower levels on the Tree. The elements of this prototype are *unity* (Kether) and *duality* (Chokmah-Force; Binah-Form). Unity-Kether is a point—thus it has position, but no dimension. It must gain "width" and "height" to manifest itself. From the zero-dimensional unity of the point at Kether emanated the one-dimensional line at Chokmah, which finally became the two-dimensional circle of Binah.

We are certainly playing around with ideas and using a lot of imagination. But what does that matter if, by using these methods on the bare structure of the Tree, we can get insights that might otherwise have been denied us? If the universe is an idea in the Mind of God then we, who are made in the image and likeness of God, might as well go and do likewise!

Well, returning to the Tree as a glyph of the universe, the next significant grouping of the sephiroth is Chesed-Geburah-Tiphareth. Once again we have a triangle, but this time it is down-pointing. Again it is the action of complementaries—this time Chesed and Geburah—that produces a new condition. But this triangle is a reflection of the first. Originally, out of unity came duality. Now the elements of the duality, Chesed and

Geburah, conjoin and from their union the new unity of Tiphareth is born. There is one reality; all else is images and reflections.

Now this second triangle has added another dimension to the simple condition of the first triangle. The circle has become the sphere. Being a reflection, the polarities are reversed; Chesed carries the "form" idea, while Geburah represents the dynamism. Tiphareth is the equilibrium of the two and embodies the essence of the *next* phase.

Again the process is repeated, once more in a triangular relationship, this time in Netzach-Hod-Yesod, a reflection of the previous pattern. The polarity is again reversed. Netzach is the dynamic partner this time, while Hod represents the "form." Yesod is the product of their interaction. In that respect, Yesod is like Tiphareth, but on a lower arc. Once again, the phases of action, reaction, and stability have resulted in a new development. The skeletal framework of forces and subtle form has been clothed with a sort of "pre-matter." Evolution has reached what occultists would call the astral plane.

From the harmony of Tiphareth came Netzach, pure elemental force. As in the first triangle, force restrained gives rise to form. In occult terms, Hod is the world of astral form in the same way as Binah is the place of "spiritual" form. Yesod is the resultant condition, not only of this triangle, but of the entire Tree. It seems fitting therefore that Yesod should bear the titles *the treasure house of images* and *the machinery of the universe*, the latter title providing a compelling picture of the controlling life behind the phenomena of the physical world.

Finally, on its own at the base of the Tree, is Malkuth, the final sephirah. It represents the physical world of matter that we know as houses, cars, trees, mountains and stars. In Malkuth is the final stage of the descent into matter. Malkuth is the lowest point on the great arc of evolution. If Kether has within it the idea of all created life, infolded like the oak in the acorn, then Malkuth represents life's most complete expression. If Kether is the alpha of the universe, then Malkuth is its omega. "I am the alpha and the omega," saith the Lord.

By using the Tree this way, we gain some idea of the method of qabalistic philosophy. Remember, at this stage we are just using the Tree as a framework, a hat stand on which to hang ideas. Notice that the method involves the creative imagination, cross-checked against the polarizing patterns of the Tree. Always remember that the Sephiroth represent *patterns* of relationship— *never fixed symbols* of things or states of being.

The Return Process

Finally, let us look briefly at the Tree as a diagram of the return process. The lightning flash (or the flaming sword, as it is sometimes called) indicates the successive order of emanation, one from the other, of the sephiroth. Each is infolded in its predecessor like the plant within the seed, right back to the uni-cellular glory of Kether. The Tree can be thought of as a diagram representing the entire scheme of creation, held in the unconscious mind of God.

All life obeys the cyclic law: after involution comes evolution. Life, having involved to its greatest capacity of complexity, withdraws sphere by sphere from the forms it has created, bearing within it the capacities developed during its stay in matter. At this point it would be well to remember that technically *all* the spheres below the first triangle represent material states. Only the supernals represent the structure of life, or form itself.

Western Qabalists maintain that we withdraw to subtler planes as we master the lessons of matter and so, ultimately, will creation itself. The "Big Bang" or explosion at the beginning of the phase starts everything; while an equivalent "implosion" withdraws all creation to a point at the end of the cycle. To represent this path of return of mankind and the universe, the glyph of the serpent Nechustan is placed upon the Tree (see figure 6 on page 28).

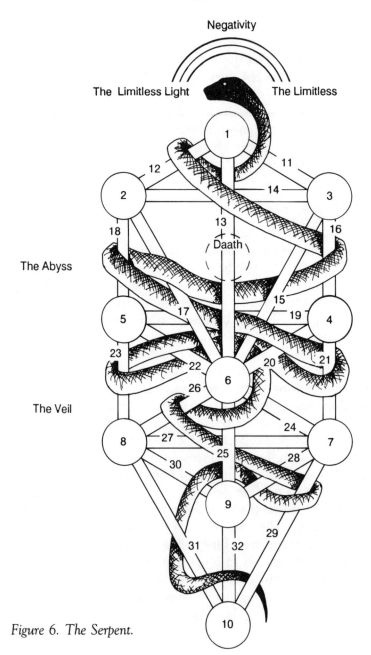

Figure 6. The Serpent.

This serpent of wisdom is so coiled about the Tree that its body passes over each path in succession on the way of return. With its tail near Malkuth and its head by Kether, it indicates the correct order of numbering the paths upon the Tree. This was once a secret reserved only for the initiated.

Students of modern qabalism do not try to "understand" the Tree in an intellectual fashion; they make it part of their inner life.

Sephirotic Relationships

Each sephirah is a factor in its own right but it can only be properly understood as part of a greater whole, as one element, in a pattern of relationships. There are a number of important patterns within the structure of the Tree which may be thought of as sub-systems within the main system of the glyph itself. The patterns are as follows:

1) Triangles: The first of these groupings has already been mentioned, the triangles. Kether, Chokmah and Binah form the supernal triangle. These first three sephiroth indicate stages of a phase of development in the universe or in humankind. Triangle Number One represents the roots of existence if the Tree is taken as a symbol of manifestation, or the roots of life if viewed as representing the soul.

The second triangle, comprising Chesed, Geburah, and Tiphareth, is often considered as a reflection of the first—inverted and reversed. The left-hand sephirah, Geburah, is the dynamic partner in this case. The right-hand sphere, Chesed, is the formalizer. Their completion is in the sixth sephirah, Tiphareth, the result of their interaction, and the source of the next phase. The second triangle is often called the ethical triangle, because it depicts the development of "law and order." In the universe this implies the emergence of what will later show forth as the "laws of nature." The equivalent in mankind is the beginnings of consciousness, the sense of right and wrong, and the concept of choice.

Netzach, Hod and Yesod—forming the third and last triangle—represent further development toward manifestation as we understand it. Although the third triangle is down-pointing (as was the second), the polarity of its complementaries is again reversed. Netzach, on the right, is positive, while Hod is formative. The sephirah Yesod represents the synthesis of the triangle and the origin of the next phase. This third trinity is often called the magical triangle. Magic has been defined as the science and art of making forms for the invocation, focusing and control of spiritual forces. Netzach represents pure elemental energy—in nature or in people—Hod is the formalizing influence, the plan in the mind of God, or concrete ideas in the minds of people. The form-making operation of Hod has made channels for the forces of Netzach. Yesod is the womb from which they are born into the material world of Malkuth, the kingdom.

Mental indigestion will result from giving too much attention to the intellectual significance of these patterns on the tree. Understanding will come from realizing their meaning in our personal lives.

2) *The Four Worlds:* Classical qabalism considered four *worlds* or conditions of being, from concept to end-result:

the World of *Atziluth*	Archetypal	the Concept
the World of *Briah*	Creative	the Detailed Plan
the World of *Yetzirah*	Formative	the Working Out
the World of *Assiah*	Material	the Result

This is a very useful way of thinking about any creative process, in mankind or in the universe.

There are two ways in which this concept can be used. First, the Tree can be divided vertically. Kether then represents the atziluthic world while Chokmah and Binah represent the creative world, Briah. The next six sephiroth form Yetzirah. Malkuth represents Assiah, the world of physical matter. The second method of using the worlds is a logical extension of the first. If the Tree can be viewed in a fourfold way, then so can any part of it. Thus, each sephirah can be thought of in four ways: the possibility; the idea; the working out; and the result—or, Atziluth, Briah, Yetzirah and Assiah.

3) The Reflections: A further and very useful way of regarding the Tree is to view the seven lower sephiroth as forming three patterns of reflection, one pattern from each of the three supernals. Aleph, Mem and Shin are the three mother letters. Aleph is called the *root of the powers of air,* and is applied to Kether. Mem is called the *root of the powers of water* and assigned to Binah. Shin is known as the *root of the powers of fire* and allotted to Chokmah. The influence of Aleph-Kether reflects downward through Tiphareth and Yesod into Malkuth. Mem-Binah reflects diagonally to Chesed and thence into Hod. Shin-Chokmah reflects across to Geburah and from there into Netzach. These are useful hints about the way the forces operate. (See figure 7a on page 32.)

4) The Hexagram: Another way of patterning the sephiroth is to consider the Tree dynamically. The first triangle is seen as the source which focuses its influence and power at a position midway between Tiphareth and Kether. This focus makes a phantom sephirah which the rabbis called *Daath* or knowledge. Malkuth is on its own at the bottom of the diagram. The central sephiroth are considered as the functional parts of this diagram, and are seen as the points of a six-sided star or hexagram. Daath makes the top point and acts as a channel from the supernal triangle, while Yesod (as the bottom point) feeds into Malkuth. This method of grouping the sephiroth stresses the sixth sephirah, Tiphareth, as the functional center of the Tree like a sun, with sephiroth 4, 5, 7, 8 and 9 arranged like planets around it. (See figure 7b.)

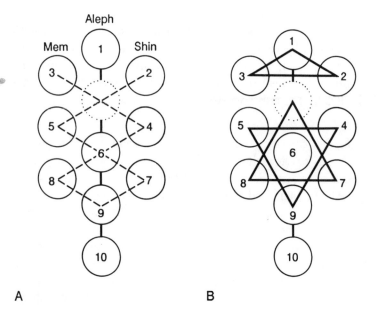

A   B

Figure 7. The Reflections (A) and the Hexagram (B).

5) *Astrological Attributions:*   Later we shall be looking at the way the astrological planets can be assigned to the Tree, so the diagram may then make more sense to those interested in the astrological symbolism.

CHAPTER THREE

The Tree and Its Forces

THE TREE OF Life is a diagram representing all the forces and factors operating within the universe and mankind. There is no characteristic, influence or energy which is not capable of representation on the Tree. The beginning, the ending and the ways between are all depicted. Thus one may see the past, the present and the future in the ten sephiroth and the twenty-two paths connecting them.

We are, by nature, form-builders. All our past has been spent in coming to grips with form; for even the airy realms of the mental plane are turgid and restricting to the spirit. It is not surprising, therefore, that the personality—itself a complex mental and emotional form—sees abstract forces in concrete symbols. God made humans in His image and likeness; and we do the same to our inner world—our perception of abstract forces is personified or formalized according to the level of our understanding at the time.

The Titans, the Olympians and the animal-headed gods of Egypt are manmade forms. Archangels, angels, seraphim and cherubim, the elementals, and the fairy folk are personified into winged forms, dwarfs, fiery wheels, pillars of fire, and so on, according to the depth of our perception and the limits of our stock of mental imagery. Personalized symbols are like words in the occultist's vocabulary. Like the words we use in daily life, they *represent* realities; danger threatens only when they are mistaken for the realities they represent.

Occultism can never be reduced to sets of rigid formulae. Human experience is individual and aspects of it may be unique. No two people respond to an experience the same way. Therefore there is little point in getting a book on the Qabalah with a convenient set of attributions and using it as a substitute for personal experience. A book can only serve to point the way. For this reason, the sections which follow are deliberately general, and the text, when specific, should be taken as suggestive, not dogmatic. In any case, everything depends upon your use of the Tree as a master-symbol.

The Gods

Our early ancestors personified the forces which they perceived within themselves and in the world around them. The more thinking members of early races speculated upon origins and upon cause and effect and upon our inter-actions with our environment. From these riches of imagery and thought came the pantheons of the gods. The average person regarded them as super-beings of super-virtue (and sometimes vice!); but to the enlightened, they were representations of forces and factors in humanity and in the universe.

All creator-gods, of whatever pantheon, can safely be assigned to Kether, the first sephirah. Force-gods, representing raw power in action, primordial dynamism, could be placed upon Chokmah, while the concept of form-building, giving birth, or archetypal motherhood depicted by the great mother-goddesses, can be associated with Binah. From this great trinity of concepts originates all that follows.

Chesed represents the concept of order and the sort of harmony that comes from civilization in its real sense, as an exercise in perfected co-operation and, quite literally, good-will. Chesed is the perfect administrator of the invisible reality, and could be thought of as the first manifestation of the "perfect plan." In humans, this sphere represents an aspect of the higher self, that part which gives form to the will of the spirit. From all this, it follows that the gods attributed to Chesed will be figures representing force in balance, wise and benevolent government and the higher ideals of order.

Geburah is complementary to Chesed. Its principles are those of holy war—again in the absolutely literal sense. Any warrior god dedicated to the destruction of evil and outworn forms can be assigned to Geburah. One title of this sephirah, Pachad (fear), is sometimes misunderstood. Cruelty and fear of violence have no place in this sphere, for they are evils. Pachad (in the opinion of this writer) means fear of the law, for fear of the law is the beginning of wisdom when "fear of" is interpreted as "respect for" the right and might of God or of the spirit of humanity. Geburah is a great initiator because it destroys in order to make way for the true works of the spirit.

Tiphareth is the reconciler of Geburah and Chesed and is sometimes called Beauty. Beautiful it is, this sphere of Shemesh, the sun, but not "pretty." Its glories are those of the sun, its symbol, and its harmony comes from the equilibrium of incredible forces. It is also the sephirah of true sacrifice, which is the transmutation of force from one level to another. To this sphere are the healing gods assigned.

This may seem strange until the implications of the foregoing are considered. Healing is "making whole," the balancing up of an unequilibrated system, and this invariably implies sacrifice of one sort or another; whether to the knife of the surgeon or the probings of the psychiatrist makes little difference. The healing of the soul, or regeneration, if you prefer it, is another important example when glamor and illusion are consumed in the sun of Tiphareth and transmuted into spiritual gold, thus "making whole" the soul of humanity.

In the last triangle on the Tree the gods symbolize things nearer to our normal understanding. Netzach depicts perfect relationship horizontally—between people, forces or mechanisms; or vertically—between one level of manifestation (or awareness) and another level. Thus the gods of Netzach are gods of polarity. Venus and Aphrodite are goddesses of love in the Roman and Greek pantheons respectively. But the true interpretation of the symbolism is in terms of polarity on all levels—not merely the physical level of sex.

In Netzach is also the "Lamp of Occult Knowledge," a symbol which represents the accumulated wisdom of humanity in its age-long search for Light. This may be confusing until the diagonal reflections across the Tree are considered. Chokmah reflects from Geburah into Netzach, which fact may reveal to the occult student another aspect altogether.

Hod is generally considered to be formal and mental in its structure, in contrast to the emotional appearance of Netzach. If Netzach represents the unconscious, emotional and artistic drives, then Hod symbolizes the conscious, mental and scientific approach to life. It is for this reason that Hod is linked with formal magic—ceremonial occultism.

Any operation which brings through a force by "feeling with" it (sympathetic induction) could be attributed to Netzach: any ceremonial invocation or evocation, whether in the Christian mass or the initiation ceremony of an occult lodge, is an operation of the sphere of Hod. However, there are vast depths to each sephirah which cannot be dealt with in this book. After all, each sephirah is an aspect of God. Hod receives the diagonal reflections of Chesed, which transmutes the force of Binah. Hod transmutes the influence of primordial water, as Netzach manifests the primordial fire. Hod's formality is not the empty regimentation of ritual for ritual's sake, but the force of the great Mother of Form itself. The gods of Hod are symbols of formalized energy. Mercury, Hermes and Thoth are all Lords of Magic, masters of the skills of science, great teachers and messengers.

All these influences pass into the ninth sephirah, Yesod, the sphere of the moon, region of the great but hidden world of the causes immediately behind the physical life. Because of the unimaginable strength of this foundation of life, Titanic gods and heroes can be assigned to this sephirah; Atlas and Heracles are two obvious choices. Lunar gods (and particularly goddesses) also are attributed to Yesod. The moon traditionally rules the underworld of the etheric, whose inner tides answer the call of the moon, as do the tides of the sea. The moon has many phases, and Hecate—mistress of witchcraft and sterility—rules over the dark phase even as the bright and fertile aspects of Isis or the ever-virgin Diana rules over the bright phases.

As in all spheres on the Tree, students should assign gods to Yesod according to their understanding of the sephirah and the god; and, as they advance, it is hoped that their understanding will deepen. For example, Pan can be assigned to Chokmah, Yesod, Netzach or Malkuth according to which aspect of the god is considered. There is a great difference in altitude between the male potency of the universe in Chokmah and the more homely woodland Pan in Malkuth. As for the great female power, she appears in innumerable forms. After a certain point is reached, formal instruction is of little use and experience is the only true guide.

Finally, Malkuth is the terminal sephirah of the Tree. If Kether is the alpha, then Malkuth is the omega. But evolution is cyclic, not linear. Malkuth represents not so much the last link of a chain as a point on a circle. Those occult students whose misunderstandings have led them to think that matter is evil might consider the words, "I am the alpha *and the omega,* saith the Lord." Malkuth symbolizes the physical universe and the gods and goddesses epitomize its characteristics. Some are gods of fruitfulness, others are of the ancient forces of the earth that made the rocks and rivers, mountains and seas. Demeter and Ceres, goddesses of the corn, Vulcan of the subterranean forge, the sylvan Pan and the bright and fertile Isis are all attributable to Malkuth.

Many occultists have turned away from Christianity and concentrated exclusively on Hebrew godforms and the pagan pantheons. Some even denigrate the Christian message as "suitable only for the masses." It is difficult to deal with ignorance of

this magnitude; probably it is a matter of growth, for what finer
and more complete exemplification of Malkuth is there than Jesus
Christ in His aspect as the supreme yet archetypical human?

The Archangels and Angels

Centuries of use by initiates of the Western Tradition have constructed many systems of symbolism around the Tree and its
sephiroth. But when the Qabalistic Tree and its system were first
written down, they comprised little more than a diagram and
certain basic attributions. The Hebrew system is, of course, rigidly
monotheistic; the pantheon of gods is replaced by ten archangels
and ten choirs of angels.

The doctrine of the four worlds has been mentioned. The
force of the deity itself operates in the Atziluthic World; that of
the archangels operates in the World of Briah; and the angelic
choirs are the divine representatives in Yetzirah; while in the
World of Assiah, the plane of physical matter, creation is epito-
mized in the form of eight planets and two cosmic conditions.
The planets should be regarded in an astrological sense rather
than as physical objects. Some of the attributes associated with
the sephiroth derive from the astrological characterization of the
planets. Critical scrutiny of the astrological definitions can give
the student additional insight into the meaning of the sephirah
in personal evolution. But it should be understood that the astrological attributions form only part of the total significance of a
sephirah.

Each sephirah also comes under the presidency of one of the
ten Holy Names of God. Some names will be familiar from the
Old Testament. Each name is a formula in its own right, and a
most fruitful subject for contemplation and meditation. The
names are listed in Table 3.

The archangels are generally considered to be great beings
perfected in an earlier phase of evolution. The angels have names

Table 3. The Ten Holy Names of God

Sephirah	Name	Meaning
1	Eheieh	I Am (or I Become)
2	Jehovah	God (The Word)
3	Jehovah Elohim	God (The Creator)
4	El	God (The Lord)
5	Elohim Gebor	The God of Battles
6	Aloah Va Daath	God Manifesting in the Higher Mind
7	Jehovah Tzabaoth	The Lord of Hosts
8	Elohim Tzabaoth	The God of Hosts
9	Shaddai el Chai	The Almighty Living God
10	Adonai Melekh, Adonai Ha Aretz	The Lord Who Is King The Lord of Earth

whose translations can be very informative. These beings are probably best thought of as intelligent complexes of the forces of the spheres with which they are associated. Each angelic type has a precisely limited function, a specialized action-reaction complex. The archangels and angels associated with the 10 sephiroth are shown in Table 4 on page 40.

Finally, the mundane terminals of the sephirotic forces—their symbols in the World of Assiah—are listed here:

1) Primum Mobile—First Swirlings

2) The Zodiac

3) Saturn

4) Jupiter

5) Mars

6) The Sun

7) Venus

8) Mercury

9) The Moon

10) The Earth

An encyclopedic knowledge of Qabalistic symbolism is of little use on its own. What is *written* here is suggestive and indicative only. What is *needed* is an intuitive knowledge of the inner significances of the symbolism and its relevance to life. This is the true Qabalistic Wisdom; it can only be developed by experience.

Table 4. Archangels and Angels Associated with the Tree

Sephirah	Archangel	Angel
1	Metatron	Chaioth ha Qadesh— Holy Living Creatures
2	Ratziel	Auphanim—Wheels
3	Tzaphkiel	Aralim—Thrones
4	Tzadkiel	Chasmalim—Brilliant Ones
5	Khamael	Seraphim—Fiery Serpents
6	Raphael	Malachim—Kings
7	Haniel	Elohim—Gods
8	Michael	Beni Elohim—Sons of the Gods
9	Gabriel	Kerubim—The Strong Ones
10	Sandalphon	Aschim—The Souls of Fire

The Paths

The ten sephiroth and their twenty-two interconnecting paths make up the "32 Paths of Glory" which constitute the Tree of Life. If the sephiroth depict conditions of existence in macrocosm, and states of consciousness in the microcosm, what then are the paths? Probably the best way to consider them is as sequences of experience. Suppose a solution of sugar is crystallized out. The first condition is liquid; the final condition is solid. The sequence of experience which the components would undergo during the change of state represents the path between solid and liquid states. The same idea applies to the sephiroth on the Tree.

Those paths that are aligned with the Lightning Flash have a special significance because they represent the "sequence of experience" undergone in the involutionary stage of matter and consciousness. The other paths can probably be best considered as depicting the sequences of experience in human awareness as it evolves from one state of consciousness (or sephirah) to another.

It is probably best to postpone undue speculation on the nature of the paths until some measure of experience is gained. However, there is no doubt that the paths, in their subjective aspect, represent collective experience in the evolution of the soul; and as such are clearly involved with certain types of practical occult work.

Supernal Paths

The most abstract level of the Tree is the first triangle of Kether, Chokmah and Binah. From this it naturally follows that the paths interconnecting these sephiroth must be of fundamental significance. The mighty experience-tracks which represent primal involution in the universe and the dawnings of consciousness in the soul depict the innermost structure of existence.

Paths 11, 12 and 14 link the supernals into the primal triangle, and of these three, paths 11 and 14 are aligned with the

Lightning Flash and so are of particular significance. The 13th path is often considered as holding the key to the exalted mysticism which unites the soul (depicted by the central sephiroth) with its spiritual source in Kether. This path, together with the 15th, 16th, 17th and 18th paths, links the triangle of spirit to the world of the soul.

Ethical Paths

Chesed, Geburah and Tiphareth form what might be called an ethical triangle, representing the higher activities of the soul. Paths 19, 20 and 22 define this triangle and paths 19 and 22 are in line with the Lightning Flash. The idea of the abstract mind is clearly connected with this triangle.

Tiphareth, in its central position on the Tree, is both a focus and distributing point. From this sephirah ray out lines of connection to the more concrete aspects of the soul, the 24th, 25th and 26th paths. Of these, the 25th path is of special note as it represents, together with the 13th path mentioned earlier, and the last path, the 32nd path, the inner core of consciousness of the Tree, the great road to the Light, the paths of Saturn (32nd), the Desert (25th) and the High Priestess (13th).

Magical Paths

It is in the lower regions of the soul that the operations of "magic" take place. Magic is a series of techniques (nothing more) designed to build structures or forms to channel force from the "higher" levels of the Tree into the material world. If the direction of the force is in line with evolution, then the magic is white; if not, it is black.

The sephiroth Netzach, Hod, and Yesod form this triangle, which might be called the triangle of the personality: the 27th, 28th and 30th paths define it. Again, two of the paths, the 27th and 30th, follow the Lightning Flash, and of these two, number 27 is especially important in our psychology, representing a great cross-girder of the personality.

Paths 29, 31, and 32 make junction with the terminal sephirah Malkuth. The final path, sometimes called the "terrible 32nd path" has been briefly mentioned earlier. Again, it is one of those paths aligned with the descending involutionary drive of the Lightning Flash; but it is also of great significance in the mystical evolution of the neophyte. In terms of evolution, Yesod is the next higher state to Malkuth. Therefore the 32nd path is the first of the mystical paths trodden by the initiate in his or her journey on the Path of Return. Here we make the first transition from the experience of brain-consciousness to the first knowledge of the soul. Here neophytes are warned that if they take "but one step upon this path," they "must inevitably come to the end thereof." After the 32nd path comes the experience of the desert and after that again, the empty room. Would-be initiates contemplating a fascinating and glamorous life of magical excitement should study the 16th century writings of St. John of the Cross on the Dark Night of the Soul.[3] Should they subsequently decide that this was not what they wanted, everyone would be saved a great deal of trouble!

---

[3]*Dark Night of the Soul*, by St. John of the Cross, translated by E. Allison Peers (London: Burns & Oates, 1953).

CHAPTER FOUR

Sephirotic Glyphs and Temples

SYMBOLISM IS A means to an end, not an end in itself. Statements of this sort have been made so many times by so many people that they should surely be considered as axiomatic by now; yet many student occultists still become obsessed by the outward trappings and lose sight of the reality which the symbol represents. It is a curious fact that many esoteric students who would indignantly deny that they confused themselves with their physical bodies become totally enmeshed in ritual, words of power, breathing exercises, or special postures, and don't understand the inner meaning of that which they so painstakingly represent to themselves with their paraphernalia.

Regeneration is aptly depicted as a journey and the terrain varies. Sometimes a car can be used; at others the road is a mere track that can only be traversed by foot. Occasionally, there are dangerous climbs on this journey and no doubt there may be times when a helicopter might be the best vehicle. The various methods of occultism provide transport for the journey. Chosen when circumstances demand their use and laid aside for another method when necessary, they all represent valid aids and valuable means to an end. But who—even in these days of strange gods—would confuse himself with his car?

There is a deep satisfaction in learning signs and symbols and, in the first flush of enthusiasm, it is all too easy to lose sight of the goal. A certain amount of experimentation "just to see what happens" is natural in any normal student and rarely does any permanent harm (or good, for that matter). The real thing to guard against is losing your inner way within the maze of a complex system with all its delightful mental puzzles and enigmas. In one ritual initiation, the candidate is warned not to "wander in the angled labyrinth of the lower mind." This is good counsel.

The first question a student should ask before working with the symbols of the sephiroth is "why?" At first, practice and familiarization are admirable reasons. Ultimately, however, when a working knowledge has been gained, the question of use arises. Symbols work on the inner levels and act either as energy transformers or "gateways." In the first case, repeated contact tends to build a channel between inner and outer levels, thus commencing the process of healing or making whole. In the second case, the symbol enshrines an inner truth which, when realized, removes a barrier or opens a gateway to a new level of life-experience in the student's environment. Symbols are realities in the inner world and should not be used lightly. At the same time superstition should be avoided. Symbols may enshrine tremendous truths. They may make possible the release of incredible forces—but so does the formula for Epsom Salts!

It is possible to present complex tables of sephirotic attributions where all known gods, goddesses, heroes, angels, archangels, elementals, pots, pans and even the kitchen sink are assigned to one or more of the spheres on the Tree of Life. But this would be of little use for reasons which should now be obvious. Therefore the following text merely gives the outline symbolism and leaves you to supply any secondary symbols and embellishment you feel is appropriate.

Colors and Magical Images

Traditionally, each sephirah has an associated color together with a special personalized symbol which is known as its magical image. Colors represent energy in the inner worlds. Actually, there are four separate color scales, one for each of the four "worlds": Atziluth, Briah, Yetzirah and Assiah.

In practice, the use of color is simple. The Briatic scale is appropriate for most purposes, at least in the initial stages of contact with the Tree. The four worlds may be seen as stages in creation—whether you are building a garage or a universe makes no real difference.

Atziluth: the idea

Briah: the plan

Yetzirah: the working out

Assiah: the result

The color scale of Briah is used for meditation work because it represents the plan of things before complications are encountered in the physical world. Thus the Briatic world, being perfect, is an ideal basis for mind work on the Tree. So we shall work with one set of colors as follows:

Kether: brilliance

Chokmah: pearl-grey

Binah: black

Chesed: blue

Geburah: scarlet

Tiphareth: yellow

Netzach: emerald

Hod: orange

Yesod: violet

Malkuth: citrine, olive, russet, black

In Malkuth, the circle representing the sephirah is quartered diagonally: citrine is toward Yesod; olive toward Netzach; russet toward Hod; and black is at the bottom.

The magical images, which were once kept secret from the uninitiated, are considered to sum up the essential qualities of the sephiroth. Here are the traditional forms:

Kether: an ancient bearded king, seen in profile.

Chokmah: a bearded male.

Binah: a mother figure.

Chesed: a mighty crowned and throned king.

Geburah: a mighty warrior in his chariot.

Tiphareth: a majestic king, a child, a sacrificed god.

Netzach: a beautiful naked woman.

Hod: an hermaphrodite.

Yesod: a handsome naked man—very strong.

Malkuth: a young woman, crowned and throned.

These, then, are the magical images handed down to us. But remember, the Qabalah is an evolving system. So it is a good exercise for you to find suitable modern images for these ideas. After all, times have changed; an ancient rabbi's idea of a beautiful naked woman or a very strong and handsome naked man might not be yours. Make sure your images do credit to what you consider as the essence of the sephirah. A mighty warrior in his chariot is still a very emotive image, while a tough tank commander in the turret of his vehicle may not be an adequate substitute, although it is a modern image.

The Hod image of a hermaphrodite may cause some trouble. The image meant to be conveyed is not that of a sexual anomaly or a freak, but the concept of one who has both male and female characteristics of soul—tenderness and strength, tears and toughness, mind and emotions.

Tiphareth, you will have noticed, has three images—a child, a king and a crucified god. These are three stages in the making of the adept, which will be made clear when you become one! Think about these things. Get your *own* imagination working and the Tree will come to life within you.

To use the sephirotic symbolism effectively, the symbols, names, etc., should first be collated and then considered separately. Finally, they should be assembled into a compound symbol and worked with in both contemplative and meditative modes; the aim being to develop a synthesis, an idea or "feeling" about the sphere.

Consider Tiphareth as an example: the number of this sephirah is 6; its color in the Briatic scale is yellow. It is the sphere of the sun and its traditional magical image is threefold—majestic king, child and sacrificed god. The symbols most associated with Tiphareth are the sun, the equal-armed and the calvary crosses, the cube, the truncated pyramid and the *lamen.* The lamen is a symbol traditionally worn on the chest of the adept. Number and color are primary considerations and any symbolic figure, whether mental or drawn upon paper, should be based upon them. The magical image is often of great antiquity, which frequently implies that a fundamental human experience is depicted therein. It is in a sense an archetype and that fact, together with the centuries of occult work upon it, gives most of these glyphs considerable latent power. In the case of Tiphareth, the image is a triple one and depicts three stages or levels of experience. Only one aspect at a time should be selected for work in this sephirah. There is no obligation to use all the symbols given, of course. Most people find one or two symbols to have particular significance for them while others have less; and some symbols may appear quite irrelevant. In this example, meditation and contemplation might well be concentrated upon the cross symbolism and the meanings of the truncated pyramid, which is a symbol of the adeptus minor, the traditional grade of Tiphareth. In the Western Esoteric Tradition, a grade is considered as a step on the path to the Light. Each higher grade is a step nearer reality and further from illusion.

Assembly into a glyph—a compound symbol—is a matter for personal inclination. One such glyph of Tiphareth, concentrating on the sacrificial aspect, depicts a crucifixion, with the base of the cross rising from the flat top of the truncated pyramid. The background is matte black while the outline of the pyramid and crucifix is yellow. From the crucifix, great beams of yellow light ray out to the hexagonal limits of the glyph. The whole thing is simple yet most effective. Another glyph concentrates upon the equal-armed cross, the whole enclosed in a cubic framework made up of a hexagon whose opposite points are joined by lines. Cross and pyramid are in yellow, defined in black, and radiate yellow light through the thin black lines depicting the cube. The solar symbolism is, of course, extremely strong in Tiphareth, and some effective glyphs have been constructed on this basis. A child "clothed with the sun" forms one glyph of great power, but some artistic ability is needed to make this sort of treatment properly effective. The "king" aspect of Tiphareth will call for the figure of a majestic king (which demands skill in drawing). However, it is possible to find many suitable pictures or drawings which can be cut out or traced to form the necessary figure.

Magical glyphs can be very simple in form or they can be sophisticated works of art. The one vital thing is that no part of them should ever be irrelevant.

Sephirotic Temples

Each sephirah can be considered a "home" for a particular type of energy or mode of consciousness. The ten Qabalistic foci have each been formalized, to some extent at least, by the many minds who have used them for centuries in meditation and ritual. These forms can be considered as complex three-dimensional glyphs or symbol-groups, into which the mind can enter and walk about, as it were. They are called sephirotic temples.

We are form-building animals and live in a three-dimensional world. Therefore our symbolism is three-dimensional in its most complete form. Sephirotic glyphs may be used in contemplation and meditation to tune into a force or gain a mental realization as to its nature. But sephirotic temples are used to *work with* the energies of a sphere on the Tree. In properly conducted work with such a form, you can build up the details of the temple in your mind's eye and then mentally enter into your form, contact its force and use it.

The purpose of a temple is worship, which is defined as adoration and reverence. To adore is "to regard with utmost respect and affection." To revere something (or someone) means to hold it (or that person) in great esteem, and in religious usage this often implies that the respect is held for something sacred (which itself means "reserved" or "dedicated" for some purpose). From all this emerge the ideas of reservation, respect and love. A sephirotic temple is, if properly built up on the inner levels, a place reserved, dedicated, or set aside for a special purpose. Love and respect are modes of comunication, means whereby the love and honor inherent in everyone can contact and be contacted by their cosmic counterparts. A temple, then, is a communication center, and each of the ten sephirotic temples is dedicated to communication of a particular type.

Much of the detail of the sephirotic temples is traditional and, at first, it is advisable to use established symbolism. Later, when more experienced, you may very well decide to design a set of symbols to suit yourself. First you should get the feel of the sephirah you are working with and use the traditional ideograms with as much intuition and sympathy as you can. In an experimental working to train a group, adepts can describe a temple in modern and, to the Qabalistic reactionary, startlingly unusual form, and it will do its work. Because the adept has experienced the force of the sphere and has a sound knowledge of its inner meaning, a temple can be constructed using a form which will convey to the group the essence of the sephirah represented. By sympathetic induction, the force can begin to flow through the image into consciousness. When this has been effectively achieved, the set of symbols composing the temple will become real and alive to the members of that group. But this is only possible for the experienced Qabalist.

Although much of your early work with sephirotic temples will concentrate upon technique, there is still a chance that you will achieve some measure of contact with the meanings and energies of the sphere in which you are working. For this reason, it is best to choose one of the sephiroth on the middle pillar to work with because each repesents a condition of balance and relative completeness.

As an example, one possible form for a sephirotic temple for Yesod is described below. These great stations on the Tree are normally approached via one of the paths. Pathworking is a highly specialized subject and the next chapter will be devoted to a brief introduction to it; therefore, for the time being, you should commence building up the image of the temple as if you were approaching it from some way off.

The Temple of Yesod Visualization

Imagine yourself as standing on a slope, looking downwards toward a lake. It is night and a crescent moon shines low on the horizon and is reflected in the waters. In the center of the lake is a small island formed out of greyish volcanic rock. On the island is the temple of Yesod. It is nine-sided and apparently formed out of quartz and rises from the grey rock like a giant crystal. The walls are luminescent with violet light and the whole temple appears as the focus of a vast aura of rainbow colors which radiate upwards in perpetual movement toward the indigo sky.

Move down the slope toward the shore of the lake where the outline of a flat-bottomed boat is visible. In the stern is dimly seen the shadowy figure of a steersman. Board the boat and the steersman will propel the craft across the lake, keeping his face turned away—like the dark side of the moon. When the rocky shore of the island is reached and you climb ashore, the boat turns to mist and its form is lost to sight.

The temple of Yesod is the temple of Lavanah, the moon, and it rests upon a small and perfectly flat plateau in the center of the island. On approaching it, the eye is half blinded by the curious dazzling opalescence of its walls, whose angles and distances appear to change bewilderingly. There seems to be no entrance, but your attention is taken by a broad vertical shaft of intense violet light, which rests upon the rocky ground and seems more solid than the ever-changing form of the walls. Looking up, you see that the shaft is in fact the lower end of a vast sword held point downward to protect the sanctity of the temple and wielded by the hand of a towering archangelic form. The eye, blinded by the brilliance and movement of the ever-changing rainbow colors that overshadow the temple, can see little. However, the impression is gained that the radiance is the aura of this great being, Gabriel, a Lord of Flame, Giver of Vision, Angel of the Annunciation and Archangel of Yesod. Violet flames now appear to emit from the blade of the great sword. They curve around you and envelope you and there is a feeling as if your soul is being probed by fingers of cool clarity. If the test is passed, the flames recede, the great sword pivots on its point, and the way into the temple is clear.

The interior is cool and dry and lit with a violet radiance which seems to emanate from the crystal walls. It is completely empty except for a black stone pillar exactly in the center. This stone, which is the altar, is about a yard high and nine-sided, like the walls of the temple. The top is perfectly flat and on it is a large moonstone supported on a silver stand. The air is fragrant with the scent of jasmine. As you stand with your back to the entrance, you are aware of a marked magnetic pull toward the altar. You move across the smooth grey floor of rock with difficulty, barely keeping your balance, and have the curious feeling that half-materialized forms are spiralling the temple, being pulled into the great focus of the altar stone.

Some of these tenuous phantoms are animal-like, some are geometrical, some are humanoid, and there are those that are combinations of all three. As you near the black stone altar, its force increases and you find yourself being moved spiral-fashion around the left side of the altar and in toward it, finally ending up at the side opposite to the door, thus facing the entrance to the temple and looking down at the great moonstone upon the altar top.

There is complete silence: a silence so profound that it seems impossible that sound could ever exist. You place your hands side by side, palms upward, on the altar top and are at once aware of a complex vibration. At first too engrossed in the sensation itself, later you are conscious that the feeling you experience outwardly imperceptibly moves within and becomes a part of your inner being. And with that realization comes a deeper awareness of the components and harmonics of the experience which now occupies your whole spectrum of livingness. This is the meaning of the temple of the moon. In this experience is condensed the essential nature of Yesod. There are deep slow rhythms pulsing like a giant heart. Profound organ notes. Great chords of feeling. Sounds like the ebb and flow of tidal water. Others chiming like a peal of many bells. And all in a totality of grand harmony contained within the framework of that deep fundamental rhythm, the living pulse-rate of the universe.

As the experience sweeps over you, you raise your eyes upward and, for a moment, are aware of the vastness of space and time. You see the stars moving with intelligent purpose in the infinity of the cosmic void, and your experience is organic and not intellectual. Atlas, the Titan, supports the rolling world and the cosmos is the living body of Adam Kadmon.

The experience continues to intensify, but you lower your eyes. You have seen as much as you can endure at this time. Later, you may return again. Mentally you give thanks for the experience and move around the altar to the left and cross the expanse of the temple toward the entrance. Although still strongly aware of the spiralling force and of the myriad forms borne upon it, you feel an inner response to the purpose of the temple and make your way without difficulty. The sword-blade moves aside and you leave the temple.

As you make your way down through the rocks to the lake-shore, you see the shadowy boat materializing out of the mist. You board it, and the dark steersman rapidly returns you to the far shore. You climb the slope, take one backward look at the temple—behind which the moon is now setting—and mentally bid it farewell. The vision fades and you return to your room in Malkuth.

· · ·

It must be stressed that this visualization is but one of many possible forms for this particular temple. However, it does demonstrate some of the basic principles involved in such a construction. You should analyze the form and its accompanying description, and attempt to define these principles for yourself.

CHAPTER FIVE

The Qabalistic Paths
& Pathworkings

I F THE SEPHIROTH are states of being, then consciousness, as our vehicle of perception of these states, needs to change in order to operate in each new condition. The paths symbolize the change in consciousness needed to perceive and function in a different dimension.

Each path joins two sephiroth. The beginning of a path partakes of the nature of its originating sephirah while its end is conditioned by the sphere to which it joins. Using the analogy of crystallization, the early state of the liquid is fluid while the penultimate state tends toward solidity. Primary and secondary symbols are both associated with each path.

Primary Symbols

Primary symbols embody the main characteristics of a path. There are three such symbols: one of the twenty-two tarot trumps; one of the twenty-two Hebrew letters; and a zodiacal, planetary or elemental sign.

Tarot Trumps

The origin of the tarot cards is uncertain and has been the subject of much speculation. Suffice it to say that these ancient and curiously evocative pictures are traditionally assigned to the Tree. Many occultists have been brought up, as it were, to regard them as an integral part of Qabalistic symbolism. The minor cards of the tarot deck are assigned to the sephiroth themselves; but our concern here is with the so-called Major Arcana, the tarot trumps.

Each path is a continuous set of symbols: primary, secondary and "connective," which normally start in one sephirotic temple and finish at or in the second sephirotic temple. The tarot trump links the first temple with the proper path. It sums up, in one glyph, the essence of the path's meaning and the forces which operate therein. Tarot symbolism is a specialized subject and beyond the scope of this work. There are many different ways of using the symbolism in work on the paths, in a ritual, and in divination. However, the imagery is so rich and evocative that I recommend that you buy a suitable book on the subject together with a deck of tarot cards for your own use. Some gentle reading and cogitation on the symbolism of the cards will do more good than formal exercise on the subject at this stage. Probably the best book for the student is Paul Foster Case's *The Tarot*, published by Macoy. Another useful book is *The Royal Road*, by Stephan A. Hoeller, published by The Theosphical Publishing House. As for tarot decks, there are many. One of the best known is the Rider pack, but choice of deck is a very individual matter and it is always advisable to select the set you personally find the most attractive.

Hebrew Letters

Each of the twenty-two Hebrew letters is assigned to one of the paths. The first letter, Aleph, belongs to the first path (11th) and the last letter, Tau, to the last path (the 32nd). Each letter is an ideogram. For example, the letter Daleth (4) means "a door," and Shin (300) represents a tooth or a serpent's fang. Each letter is said to have divine significance, a power in its own right. Holy writ meant literally that to the ancient Hebrews. Each letter had enfolded within it a power of the Breath of God, as it were. And the numeric value of a letter (there were no separate symbols for numerals) was considered as having significance within a grand cosmic numerology (see Table 1 on page 20).

Treading the paths of the Tree in the imagination—whether working alone, with other members of a group, or ritually—is called "pathworking." The tarot trump sounds the key-note of the path and comes at its beginning, whereas the Hebrew letter is encountered at the half-way mark of the journey and represents the focus of the forces of the path.

The Signs

In the course of its use by mystics and magicians through the ages, the tree has gathered about itself many systems of symbolism. Among these, imagery from alchemy and astrology provides the third and last of the primary symbols. The twelve zodiacal signs, the seven planets (Saturn, Jupiter, Mars, Sol, Venus, Mercury and the Moon) together with the alchemical symbols of air, fire and water, constitute a set of twenty-two symbols, one for each path. Each of these symbols is rich in imagery and evocative of ideas.

Many students of astrology have learned that some astrological signs and planets are malefic. The philosophy of the Tree requires that the student understand the real meaning of the so-called bad symbol; for when it is understood, it is no longer a malefic influence. The sign comes at the end of the path and is traditionally encountered before access is gained to the next sephirotic temple. Properly understood, it represents the summation of the path's influence on the student who truly treads it in life, not merely in meditation.

Secondary Symbols

The secondary symbols comprise what might be called the flora and fauna of the path—conditions and symbolic devices traditionally associated, such as precious stones and perfumes. A path on the Tree is not like a concrete road with the three major symbols arranged symmetrically upon it. Rather it has the continuity of natural imagery, the secondary symbols serving to tune the mind toward realization of the three great primaries, with other connective description serving to link the whole together into a single continuously unfolding experience. The major secondary symbols are six: animals, plants, precious stones, color, condition, and perfume. A seventh set of symbols, the "magical weapons," are beyond the scope of a simple introduction such as this.

The student should always remember that, like the sephirotic symbolism, tradition is a good servant, but a limiting and constraining master. This applies particularly to the secondary symbolism of the paths. If a symbol does not appeal, don't use it. An example of a set of symbols for a path might help to illustrate this:

Path 25,	*The desert*	*(joining Yesod and Tiphareth)*
Primary Symbols:	Tarot trump:	Temperance (No. 14)
	Hebrew letter:	Samekh
		(a prop—value 60)
	Sign:	Sagittarius (a fire sign)
Secondary Symbols:	Animal:	Centaur, horse, dog
	Plant:	the rush
	Stone:	Jacinth
	Color:	Blue
	Condition:	Hot and dry
	Perfume:	Aloes

Clearly, a great number of effective path descriptions could be constructed around this basis. But the most effective one would be that which most powerfully and simply evoked the essential spirit of the path. Pathworkings operate upon the psychology of the *operator*; it is superstition to think otherwise. But, if the symbolism does its work, then the unconscious levels of the mind, themselves, may contact the macrocosmic forces of the path.

To conclude this brief introduction to the Qabalistic paths is an example of a simple form of the 32nd path. It is important to note that if any path is followed, whether in solitary imagination or group working, a proper return *must* be made to the sephirah from which the path originated. Failure to effect a proper return followed by full and conscious re-establishment in the physical universe can result in psychological dissociation—a dangerous and incapacitating state.

Pathworking is essentially a composition of mood. Before the path is worked through in meditation, it should be read through twice at normal speed, then twice more, but slowly. The student should carefully build the scenes described in the text. Only when completely familiar with both sequence and detail should "live" working be attempted.

The 32nd Path Visualization

(Note: The journey is probably best conducted with an invisible companion—an imaginary guide—whose presence is sensed but not seen.)

We have the impression that we are deep within the Earth. Slowly at first, there builds up around us the outline of a large cave with rock walls and a beaten earth floor, making a roughly cubical area the size of a fairly large room. From the center of the floor rises a square-cut granite pillar about waist height and with a flat top, something over a foot across.

This is the temple of Malkuth. On the top of the pillar, which is an altar, is an ancient stone lamp with a small but steady flame. Beside the lamp is an unglazed dish which contains a piece of rock crystal whose facets reflect the light of the lamp.

Between the far side of the altar and the eastern wall of the temple is a curiously carved wooden throne of archaic pattern. It is unoccupied. On the eastern wall behind the throne hangs a large tapestry depicting the life-sized figure of a dancing woman, naked except for a wind-blown veil, which covers the thighs. The figure is framed in an oval wreath of laurel leaves. The woman carries two spiral rods, one in each hand. The spirals twist in opposite directions and bring to mind the two complementary forces which are the foundation of mankind and the universe. At the corners of the tapestry are depicted the heads of the four holy living creatures. In the top left corner is the head of a man; at the top right, the head of an eagle; the bottom right bears the head of a lion; and in the bottom left corner is the head of a bull. These are the analogues on a higher plane of the four alchemical elements of air, water, fire and earth which together form the basis of Malkuth, the kingdom. At the bottom of the picture, like an archaic letter "n" is the Hebrew letter "tau," whose influence governs the 32nd path. This whole picture of the 21st tarot trump has a compelling reality about it which occupies our attention for some time.

Suddenly, the light in the cavern gets brighter. The flame of the altar light is growing larger every second and is surrounded by innumerable darting particles of many-colored intense light. These are the outer forms of the Aschim, the souls of fire, the inner energies of the sphere of Malkuth. The flame now reaches the rocky roof of the cave which appears to melt away revealing the velvet darkness of a star-studded indigo sky. The seven stars of the Great Bear glitter coldly in the void and, as we watch, the flame soars into the infinity of space and seems for a moment to make junction with Polaris, the Pole Star, shining immediately above the cave.

There is a brief but intense impression of the unity of all things and the strength of the inner world of Malkuth. We are also aware of the presence of a being and realize that we are in the presence of the archangel of Malkuth, Sandalphon. Mentally we greet this great being and ask its protection on the path.

The light slowly diminishes, and we walk around the left side of the altar, and passing behind the throne, stand before the great tapestry.

On closer examination, the picture proves to be made up of innumerable horizontal lines of modulated light, rather like the image on a television screen. From this position it is possible to see through the picture and there is the faint impression of an archway behind it. We feel drawn to pass through the tapestry to this archway which marks the beginning of the path. Moving toward the picture and slowly passing through it, we feel as if the many lines of light of which it is composed are working like some kind of sieve or filter. What emerges on the further side of the veil is the more etherealized aspects of ourselves: the grossest physical aspects have been left behind. We feel more alive, lighter in body and clearer in mind. Now we stand within the archway at the beginning of the 32nd path.

The way ahead is quite dark. The only light, which is very faint, comes from the tapestry which is now behind us. Moving cautiously forward, our feet feel a smooth path of rock leading downward, away from the temple of Malkuth. It is now quite dark, yet the sky above is not black, but deepest indigo; and on looking down we see that our bodies are surrounded by a faint greyish and misty light. We proceed on our way by these lights— our own lights.

The air is dry but cold, and the way gets steeper. Under foot are now rough rocks and, sometimes, dangerously loose scree. On either side of the way, walls of rock begin to close in on us until finally they can be touched by our outstretched hands, and the sky is only a narrow slit of intense indigo far above.

We battle on down the seemingly endless track, stumbling over stones and slipping on scree until, after what seems an infinity of time, the path seems less steep and the way smoother. The rock walls recede slowly and quite suddenly the path flattens out and widens, and we stand at the entrance to a small rock-enclosed plateau.

Now it is quite light enough to see. Pausing for a moment, we see before us a sparse grove of ivy-covered oak trees. We move toward the trees and, as we enter the grove, we hear the distant bellow of a bull. The trees are gnarled and ancient and, on passing through them, we feel the weight of aeons pressing upon us as if everything were frozen in a perpetual moment of the past.

The light is brighter now as we pass out of the trees toward the center of the plateau, but a cloud of mist hangs over us and prevents us from discovering the source of the light. In the center of the rock-strewn earth of the clearing stands a tall, solitary cypress tree; its branches shine silver-white in the light which shines down from directly above it, making a halo in its passage through the thinning mist. Nothing moves. The light slowly intensifies; we stand looking up at the tree.

Slowly there comes upon us a feeling as if some vast and silent presence, the spirit of this place, was slowly concentrating in the area around the cypress and ourselves. The light, too, is changing its form, and now seems to spotlight the tree and the space around it: all else is in profound darkness.

The awareness of the presence grows in us. It is as if we were being wrapped about in a mantle of infinity. Past, present and future become fused into one time and a single splendid certainty. And, at the height of this experience, we raise our eyes to the source of the light and see now its point of origin, a vast image of the Hebrew letter "tau" high in the indigo darkness of the sky above our heads. The letter is rather like a small "n" burning with a soft white radiance.

The experience slowly diminishes in intensity and the tau symbol gradually withdraws into the sky.

Once again, we move on. The far end of the plateau gives onto a broad and gently sloping path leading downwards. Above our heads the sky is now filled with stars which cast a faint light upon the smooth and easy road ahead. The way now levels off for a while, then gently rises. Ahead of us is a low ridge, its dark crest rimmed with a faint silver light. We climb slowly up the gentle slope toward the increasing light at the top. Our eyes, dazzled by the unaccustomed glare, are confused, but for a moment just before the crest, the figure of the ancient god Saturn—rather like Old Father Time with his scythe—seems to stand on the way before us. He vanishes as we reach the top of the ridge.

Before us the ground falls away to the shores of a lake. The crescent moon hangs over a small and rocky islet set in the lake. On the island stands the temple of Yesod, a nine-sided structure apparently formed of crystal. Shining with its own light—a violet radiance—it is encompassed by the aura of a vast being whose outstretched wings fill the sky before us. This is the vision of the archangel of Yesod, Gabriel.

We pause for a moment, trying to absorb the beauty and power of the scene. But the time has come for departure, and, after saluting Gabriel, we turn and commence the return journey.

The way is easier now and we quickly travel down the side of the ridge and up the gentle slope to the plateau. The light is stronger, partly due, perhaps, to the clear starry sky, partly to the increased light that our own bodies radiate. Quickly crossing the plateau, past the still and silent cypress and through the oak grove, we start the difficult climb back to the temple of Malkuth. But this too is easier now and we manage the steep ascent with little trouble.

Soon we are back outside the temple. We pass through the veil one by one and stand before the altar. The flame from the lamp briefly surges upward, as if in recognition, and we give silent thanks for our safe journey.

As we stand silently before the altar, the temple of Malkuth seems to fade away and we return to full consciousness of the physical plane.

[End of Path]

CHAPTER SIX

Cosmogony

EARLIER WE CONSIDERED evolution, using the ten sephiroth as a sort of "flow diagram" to depict origins, evolution, and the end-result. Now we will look at the process in slightly greater detail. We briefly discussed the concept of evolution and purpose. It was suggested that mankind and the universe are developing from a simple and uncoordinated state to a highly developed perfection. Cosmogony is the study of this process.

We need to look at the whole question of origins and evolution. This is not just an interesting philosophical speculation—it provides the fundamentals of occult theory and practice. Without this knowledge and the basic ideas which arise from it, occultism is sheer superstition. Now don't misunderstand what we are going to try to do. We are not going to give you the "truth" about the beginning and the ending of things! No one can do that: even if we knew all the details, it would be beyond the power of words to convey the process, and beyond the power of the mind to assimilate it. As we progress in understanding, our comprehension will increase. The explanation I shall provide seems to make sense and offers a reasonable explanation of the way practical occultism works; more than that we cannot learn at the moment.

The subject of origins is a very abstract one. When talking about the Tree of Life we connected Kether with this idea. But

Kether is just a symbol whose only purpose is to help us come to grips with a very abstract concept. It is all too easy to suppose that if you know the words then you must understand the idea. Not so. Words are just symbols for the idea being put forward. Words are meant to paint pictures in the mind; never to depict actual processes. Nevertheless, they do a good job because they help us to handle concepts that would otherwise be impossible to imagine.

We Westerners have developed our minds to a high degree, but in a very narrow way. We have been taught to believe that our mental capacity can be judged by the complexity of the ideas that we can manipulate and our ability to perform mental gymnastics. The mysteries of origins and endings must be mind-blowingly simple. Yet clumsy words with 3-D associations are all that we can use. So we can see that we will need to give our minds a rest and try to let the ideas sink in, rather than attempting to "understand" them. And don't confuse the symbol with the thing it is supposed to depict.

Because the concepts we are going to consider cannot easily be described, the best thing to do is to read a section and then try to feel what has been described. Don't strain at it. Re-read the material if necessary. The descriptions used are designed to train the mind rather than to inform it.

Records of processes or events normally start at the beginning. Western minds are conditioned to think in opposites. So, if there is an "end" to something, it must (we think) have a "beginning." If there is a "future," then there must be a "past," and "now" is somewhere in between. But this is just an example of the restrictions of the mind which gets all its experience from the limited three dimensional world we are focused in. We think in straight lines, beginning "here" and ending "there."

To understand the ideas in this chapter, you need to practice thinking in circles and spirals. Circles have no beginning or ending, but a cycle of out-going and return. So, whenever we are forced to use the words "beginning" and "ending," remember they are only relative terms, used simply to come to grips with the subject we are discussing.

In the pages which follow, we shall continue to use the Qabalistic symbol system to represent unthinkable thoughts! Try to get your own ideas on the subjects discussed. One original idea from you is worth two given by someone else. This book is intended as a guide and a stimulus to your own creativity, not as a brainwashing device.

Let us start by thinking big and imagining the development of the universe. Now we have to get into the act somehow, so let us imagine that this particular cycle we call the universe is about to begin; we are at that point on the circle.

Zero—No-thing

The previous cycle has ended and the new cycle has not yet begun. We have frozen the picture to examine it. So what sort of state do we find? There is nothing left of the previous cycle because it has finished; and there is nothing to be seen of the new cycle because it has not yet started. So we have a condition which must somehow contain the old cycle at the same time as all the potential for the new cycle.

But the new phase has to originate from something, surely? Yet this between-cycles state cannot be "something" because there is, as yet, no "thing" to "be." The universe cannot come forth out of nothing because there must have been something before it. So it must have come out of No-*thing*. This condition we can call the unmanifest state.

This idea is a vital one, so it is worth considering what it must imply. First, this "unmanifest" does not exist; it non-exists! If it does not exist, it cannot have any qualities; therefore, it is changeless. So it must be the most stable thing there is. In fact, it must be the ultimate stability. But it "contains" the past and also all the possibilities of the future; so it must be infinitely potent.

For us to be able to imagine it, it would have to possess qualities; but if it had qualities it would be manifest, which it is not. Therefore, it must be unimaginable. As it has no qualities, it must represent, to our minds, non-existence.

Remember again the biblical quotation: "I am the alpha and the omega, the beginning and the ending, saith the Lord; that is and was and shall be; the almighty." Now this quote may have a deeper meaning for you than it had before.

If we number the phases in the development of the universe, then this unmanifest state has to be represented by zero. Most occultists believe that we evolved in parallel with the universe. If this is true, then it follows that in each of us there is an innermost part which is unmanifest. "As above, so below."

Now take a look at the diagram of the Tree of Life. Above Kether are the three veils; negativity, the limitless, and the limitless light. These veils, out of which the entire tree manifested, represent zero, the unmanifest state, non-existence. So here is our first correlation with the symbolism of the Qabalah:

The Unmanifest State = The Three Veils of the Tree

I hope that you have found this exercise in mind-bending useful. It is important for two reasons. First, in its own right unmanifestation is a basic principle. Second, it is an example of how, by agreeing to extend ordinary words beyond their usual limits and reasoning from one concept to another, we can start the process of stretching the mind and achieve extended understanding. This is the basis of abstract thinking.

Keep the diagram of the Tree beside you for reference. Using the same sort of word-pictures as before we can continue our investigations.

Unity—the Point

If we give the value zero to the unmanifest condition, then the roots of all existence, the first moment in the life of the new universe, must rate as "one."

Imagine a focus within the unmanifest condition. Out of no-thing appears a point. If you remember your school geometry, you will recall that a point has position but no dimension. So this first dawning of creation is still not "real" to our minds because there is nothing we can really come to grips with; a point has no magnitude.

Imagine all the vastness, power and beauty of the universe that is to come, packed into a point that has no size—just a position in the vast ocean of no-thing. Using the Tree as a glyph of the development of the universe, then this condition of the primordial point is assigned to Kether, the crown, the first sephirah. So here is the second correlation with the Qabalah:

The First Point of Creation = Kether, the Crown, the first Sephirah

Two—the Line

The point is the first appearance of the universe, yet we cannot comprehend it except by symbol; it has no shape. Occultists maintain that duality is a necessity before manifestation of any-thing can occur—it takes two to tango.

In the next phase, then, a second factor is introduced—movement. The point moves and produces a line, a one-dimensional figure. But remember, the point was simply a focus in no-thing; therefore no-thing moved. This extension of the point into a line, this great cry, "Let there be Light," is called by the Qabalists, Chokmah.

The First Movement, the Line = Chokmah, the second Sephirah

Three—the Circle

The unmanifest has no properties, therefore it cannot possess inertia. Once the point moved, it went on moving. But all actions generate reactions, so the movement induced a counter-influence and this can be imagined as operating at right-angles to the original track. The results of this were to pull the line into a slight curve, leaving a vast curved track in no-thing. Eventually the circuit was complete and a colossal circle was generated, unimaginable to our minds.

This was the first boundary, the first enclosure, the first hint of the first stage of the first idea of the first two-dimensional form. This condition is called the ring cosmos. It is the end of the first phase of creation. The unmanifest has brought forth a child. This is primordial motherhood and is assigned to Binah.

The Circle, the First Idea of Form = Binah, the third Sephirah

Four to Six—the Sphere

Imagine the ring cosmos, a vast circle, spinning with a changeless spinning for aeons. But nothing remains static forever in evolution, as we have seen. Once again, action induces reaction. The forces that produced the circle must themselves invoke responses. As the ring spins, its motion gradually pulls more of the unmanifest space into itself. Finally, the spinning ring becomes a spinning disc.

Again, the condition persists for ages and again it generates another force—but this one is spectacular! In reaction to the spinning of the first ring—the ring cosmos—a second ring is generated at right-angles and "outside" the first ring. This new element is called the ring chaos.

Once more, the law of action and reaction operates. The two rings interact. The original, the ring cosmos, is attracted toward the newer ring chaos and acquires a secondary motion. The spinning ring cosmos now rotates upon its axis and becomes a spinning sphere. This new three-dimensional boundary is called the ring pass-not.

The three great rings—cosmos, chaos and pass-not—are the primary forces of this universe and *all* influences can be traced back to them. Functionally, they operate as a unit. Together they make the basic framework of the universe, the primal trinity, the three-in-one.

But don't forget that humanity is said to have evolved with the universe. So these vast forces are not remote to us. "As above, so below." Our innermost nature is bounded by the same sort of structure, in miniature, as the universe itself.

The universe in its totality is sometimes called the cosmos, from a Greek word meaning "beautiful order." It is thus contrasted with chaos, another Greek word meaning "formless," or "without order."

The development of the primal ring (the first idea of form) was symbolized by the veils—out of which all creation emerged—Kether the point, Chokmah the line and Binah the circle. These three sephiroth make up the first triangle on the Tree. Below these first three spheres, a line is drawn. This dividing mark is called the abyss. Above it are conditions so abstract as to be incomprehensible to the mind. In view of your brain-twisting work in the previous paragraphs, you will probably agree. For, remember, in "explaining" the beginnings of things I was just using symbols. Symbols enable you to come to grips with the unthinkable, in order to gain insight. But symbols *must never be confused with the reality* they represent. They are just tools.

Now, with the development of the sphere, we are below the abyss. Things are still very abstract, but at least they resemble some of the things we know. Chesed and Geburah represent the form and force side of the development of the sphere and are resolved in Tiphareth, the sixth sephirah which represents the completion of this phase.

The Framework of Three-Dimensional Beginnings = Chesed, Geburah and Tiphareth, the fourth, fifth, and sixth Sephiroth

Seven to Nine—Form

The spinning sphere with its three fundamental components is now quite a complex structure. Therefore it is not surprising that the constant interaction of the fundamentals generates new, more complex, forces. Tradition says that these interactions and re-interactions ultimately produced the basis of form as we know it.

Some of the newly generated forces are important to our understanding of the occult view of life and form; so we must give them some space. First, the interactions of the three great primaries—the rings cosmos, chaos and pass-not—give rise to a series of radii within the sphere. These radii or "rays" are vast currents of force linking the center with the circumference. They can be imagined as great figure-eight movements like highly organized convection currents in a heated liquid. This phase of the great circulating forces of the universe can be symbolized by Netzach on the Tree.

Next, remember that the sphere is actually formed by a spinning disc. Now, when a disc spins, the forces push the heavier components to the outside; in fact, they take up a position between center and circumference which depends upon their mass. So the composition of the sphere is not uniform but arranged in "layers." These layers are the cosmic planes. This stage in development, the sorting-out of pre-matter, we will equate with the eighth sephirah, Hod.

The rays, passing through the planes, react differently according to the density of the planes; and so a whole new set of forces is generated. From these complex interactions, the basis of what we call "form" is evolved. It is still far from solid, but at least the framework is there!

This ray-plane interaction forms the "astral plane" of the new universe. It is a realm of forces and tenuous pre-forms and is symbolized by Yesod on the Tree of Life.

The Framework of Form = Netzach, Hod and Yesod, the seventh, eighth and ninth Sephiroth

Ten—Dense Matter

Finally, increasingly complex interactions between the newly formed ray-plane forces give rise to increasingly complex form. The end result of this process is "matter" as we now know it. In the way we have been using the Tree for this exploration, Malkuth is the correct sephirah to represent dense matter.

The Universe of Matter = Malkuth, the tenth Sephirah

Great Entities and Divine Sparks

There is a similar organization of matter within each one of us. The most dense level we call the physical body. And in the center is the central stillness, the core of our innermost being.

Imagine a point in time after the formation of the cosmos. Units of life, nuclei of intelligent energy, now move within the vast tides of the cosmos. Some of these may be imagined as having experience in previous cosmic phases; others are but recently originated. The former are known as "great entities." By their greater "mass" they attracted lesser lives, and these, the "divine sparks," remain within the aura of a great entity for the remainder of that cosmic phase.

Consider one of these great entities, one "old" enough to have experienced all the phases of the current cosmic cycle. Having registered all the external stimuli, It now enters a subjective phase, a period of internal organization. The cosmic background is now habitual, having become part of Its being. Thus there is nothing of which to be aware: all is subjective; the great entity is aware of Itself.

The process of self-awareness develops a subject-object loop, producing an image of its own consciousness. The great entity's consciousness, being cosmos-conditioned, produces as its self-image a replica of the cosmos in miniature. Within this system are the divine sparks. These, perceiving the structure of the image, work within it, exploring its possibilities and reacting to its constraints. This process gives a degree of objectivity to the image. By their reactions the sparks evolve. From the foregoing it will be seen that:

1) The lesser lives serve the greater life while themselves evolving.

2) The great entity, while being the creator and architect of his own system, was *not* the creator of the lesser lives—the sparks. These latter, though of almost infinitely lesser stature, were of the same origin and type as the great entity.

3) Everything within the cosmos evolves; nothing is static.

These considerations form the basis of much of the occult thesis. They are, of course, merely analogies of that which is beyond description. Moreover, they are hypothetical; they may or may not be "true."

It is one of the great entities who is the creator, conditioner and sustainer to this, our solar system, and who is "God" to this system. The lesser lives, the divine sparks, are ourselves, the human race. All manifested life obeys the cyclic law. Cosmos, solar system and human beings have their negative and positive phases—birth, maturity, death and unmanifestation.

At the end of this phase of evolution, the human race will have developed to the point where it will have experienced all aspects of the great entity's image, and added another dimension to it. Thus the *group* "mass" of the human race will be, in one sense, equal to that of the great entity. In this state, two-way communication is possible and the human race will receive the fruits of the entity's cosmic experience. What this may mean to us we cannot, at our present stage, imagine.

CHAPTER SEVEN

Esoteric Anatomy

"THE PROPER STUDY of mankind is Man," said the poet. Now that we have some basic information and simple tools, it is time to study this fascinating and dangerous creature in more detail. In the early days of things, the world and people were obviously very different from what they are now. As the universe developed from a subtle system of stresses into a physical form of increasing complexity, so, says the esoteric tradition, did our bodies develop.

In each one of us a new body was developed in response to each new phase of evolution. This body, being made up of the substance of the plane concerned, enabled us to live in that phase and experience the new characteristics. So each of us is a miniature universe, and the universe is sometimes symbolized as a human being.

So, for each phase of evolution there is a corresponding level in our inner make-up. But these levels or bodies are not separate. Each is an expression of the central core, the spirit; and each body represents a functional aspect of this nature. Each of us is whole being. Each part is individual—but not separate. No one body is more important than the others. Even the spirit cannot work within the conditions of earth without a physical body.

In the beginning of this phase of evolution, the divine spark emerged with its fellows, drawn in the wake of the great entity.

Around this subtle nucleus grew the bodies of the later stages of evolution. The divine spark (or spirit) placed its stamp on all the later bodies. The spirit is the true being; thus all the later bodies should be expressions of its unique purpose.

Fundamentally, each of us is a unity and should function as such. So why are we analyzing this unity? In practice, there are two good reasons. First, because things do not always go smoothly in evolution. We have free will and can make mistakes; and we do! As a result of some of these errors in the past, "splits" have developed between the "higher" parts, which had a good idea of what should be done, and the later-developed "lower" bodies, which sometimes wanted to go their own way and developed a will of their own.

Second, because *practical*—as distinct from theoretical— occultism cannot properly be performed unless there is a clear understanding of the working and inter-connection of the bodies on the different planes. The practicing occultist must be practical. No matter how clearly you realize the essential unity and sorrow over the errors of the past, you know that you must work in the conditions which apply in the present time if you want to do something, rather than just theorizing.

In making a study of humankind, it is convenient to think of ourselves in two different ways—structurally and functionally. The study of our inner structure is called esoteric anatomy; study of our behavior is called esoteric physiology. In this chapter we are going to deal with our structure and will consider various systems used to classify our different bodies.

Systems of Classification

Twofold Classification: The first way to classify our parts is to divide the body in two:

1) Material   Body
2) Non-material   Emotions, mind and spirit

This system merely separates the being from its physical vehicle.

Threefold Classification: This method is the one familiar to Christian thought:

1) Body	Body (including brain)
2) Soul	Mind and emotions
3) Spirit	The real person

Some Christian texts merely consider soul and body, in which case "soul" includes the spiritual nature.

Fourfold Classification: This system is widely used within the Western Mysteries. It is a practical classification based on actual function. Three sub-divisions of the non-physical aspect are made:

1) Body	Body (including brain)
2) Emotions	Often called the astral body
3) Mind	Thinking and abstract mind
4) Spirit	The true human being

This is a very useful form of division, as it can be equated with the findings of modern psychology.

Sevenfold Classification: You should be familiar with this system because it is commonly employed by the Eastern Occult Tradition. In the West, we use it mostly for theoretical work. It corresponds with the seven planes of the universe and thus, with the seven bodies we gain in our evolutionary journey. From it, the fourfold system is derived by including abstract and concrete aspects of a body in one division.

1) Body	Body (and brain)
2) Concrete Emotions	Normal emotional function
3) Abstract Emotions	Higher emotional feelings
4) Concrete Mind	The normal, logical, mind

5) Abstract Mind   Abstract (non-thinking) ideas
6) Concrete Spirit   The "doing" aspect of spirit
7) Abstract Spirit   The "being" aspect of spirit

It may be helpful to look at some of these divisions more closely in order to get a clear idea of what is meant by the descriptions. Some occultists are worse than computer buffs in their use of buzzwords.

Concrete emotion involves feelings such as anger, grief, joy, desire, and so on. Abstract emotions include selfless love, devotion to an ideal and religious feelings. The concrete mind is the normal thinking, logical mind that works out problems and makes plans. The abstract mind is creative and inspirational and gets ideas that have to be described in many words. The concrete mind thinks in words; the abstract mind thinks in complete concepts and is closely related to spirit in its workings. The term "concrete spirit" may seem like a contradiction in terms; but what is really meant is the dynamic part of our essence. When we speak of "spiritual will," we are describing one aspect of concrete spirit. Abstract spirit is the very core of our being; it simply IS.

Lastly, let us look at the physical body. We have said that body includes brain, which is fairly obvious. But many people think of brain and mind as being the same thing. They are not. The brain is simply the instrument of the concrete mind, rather like a wonderful telephone exchange connected with all the parts of the body. But the mind can go on thinking and calculating and decision-making without the help of the brain. The brain is only necessary to the mind if something has to be done involving the body. If you want to write a letter or draw a diagram, then you employ your mind and the brain is needed to give the body the necessary instructions.

The molecular structure of the physical body is built up within an invisible framework, a sort of magnetic field. It is within this subtle structure, which is the vehicle of the animal life forces, that new growth and the repair that we call "healing" take place. This web of invisible forces we call the etheric body.

The Evolutionary Viewpoint

There is another way of considering humans and their bodies—from the point of view of evolution. The previous chapter briefly considered some of these ideas. Let us develop them a little. We can be thought of as spiritual beings who are immortal and eternal and who remain within this universe until we evolve to the point where we have fulfilled our destiny, our part of the great plan. When this stage is reached, the laws of the universe have become part of our nature. We have transcended the law by *becoming the law* and are now gods, evolving centers in the cosmos.

We have seen that, during each evolutionary phase, the spirit develops bodies to act as vehicles through which it can perceive and act out the conditions of that phase. When the denser levels are developed, the laws of those planes involve the conditions of "death" and "birth" as we understand them. Physical bodies are subject to the laws and conditions of the world, being made up of the material of that world. Physical bodies are subject to the stresses and strains of the highly condensed physical world and only last for a limited time. So our more subtle aspects "reincarnate" periodically in new bodies.

Now these more subtle parts of humanity cannot experience dense matter directly—only the physical body can do that—so they learn by absorbing the essence of the physical body's experience on earth. This process mostly takes place after "death."

During the material phase of evolution, these subtle parts project many physical bodies into matter and gain considerable experience in the process. They are known collectively as the *individuality*, because they embody the true human and all the experience we have gained so far in evolution. The denser parts, which actually go through the processes of incarnation and reincarnation, birth and death, are called the *personality*. Thus a *personality* embodies the experience of one life; but the *individuality* contains the experience of aeons. Using the sevenfold system of classification, the links between our anatomical and evolutionary divisions can easily be seen:

Seven fold Anatomical	Four fold Evolutionary
Abstract Spirit	Spirit, the Essential Being
Concrete Spirit	Individuality
Abstract Mind	
Concrete Mind	
Abstract Emotions	Personality
Concrete Emotions	
Body/Brain/Etheric	The Physical Being

So we now have a new fourfold division, based upon our evolution. To the personality of this life, the individuality is vast in experience, all-knowing and all-powerful. Broadly speaking, this is true, at least for the earlier work of occult development. However, the individuality may also have made some errors; it may have said "my will be done" instead of "thy will." So to abstract spirit, the individuality may appear as an erring child! All things are relative.

On the Tree of Life, we can place spirit on Kether; the individuality on Chokmah-Binah (concrete spirit) and Chesed-Geburah (abstract mind); the personality on the lower triangle of Netzach, Hod and Yesod; and the physical body on Malkuth.

You have been learning some of the jargon of Western Occultism. But definitions and classifications simply get in the way of truth if they are not used constructively. Try to make these ideas come alive by thinking them over and trying them out upon the Tree.

Psychological Relationships

By now you should have some idea of the various systems used to classify our inner nature. We have seen that, during our journey through planes of increasing density, we developed "bodies" with which to feel and act in the conditions in which we found ourselves.

As there are supposed to be seven planes in the universe, and we are apparently miniature replicas of the universe, then why not just have a seven-plane classification and avoid all the complication? Well, the reason that other systems are used is a matter of function. In practice, it is difficult to separate "abstract" and "concrete" functioning, for one usually involves the other. Thus, the practical and simple fourfold system is often used.

When a new body is developed for a particular plane, it is not a stand-alone system, but a newly acquired set of tools and the skills to use them—a further extension of the spirit's functional capacity. Not something "new," but an extension of what is already there. So perhaps you can see why it is impossible, in practice, to separate levels of consciousness or different parts of a body.

One dangerous result of the Western urge to classify everything is to build up false ideas in the mind based upon the structure of the filing system rather than the things it contains. One typical example is to imagine humanity as a vertical structure with spirit "up" and the material world "down." Unfortunately, this sort of thing reinforces childhood religious ideas when marble angels always pointed upward to a heavenland somewhere in the sky.

In reality, the "higher" planes are more accurately represented as being "within." The planes are not extended in space; they represent different ways in which the spirit can function, complex in the material world and simple in the realms of spirit. Thus you can imagine yourself as having a spiritual core with the "outermost" body as crystallized spirit. This way of thinking, although still symbolic, avoids the error of making spirit into a sort of captive balloon hovering somewhere above the head! It also permits comparisons with the valuable findings of modern psychology.

There are many psychological systems, and all of them contain something of use; but the only one that approaches the ideal of a complete scheme, one that not merely describes our inner worlds but also helps to get them in order, is the system of C. G. Jung. He built up his theory and practice from observation and practical experiment, and it is encouraging to see how close his findings come to traditional occult theory. Jung's teaching on the nature of the psyche (the inner world), its structure and the way the conscious part of ourselves relates to it, compares closely to the viewpoint of the Western Occult Tradition.

Now, for the moment, we are looking at the psyche, so the physical elements we previously discussed, including the etheric, are excluded. Bearing that in mind, our psychological parts can be represented as follows:

Emotional body

Mental body

Spiritual body

And from the evolutionary viewpoint:

Personality

Individuality

Spirit

Jung used the word "psyche" in quite a broad sense; all conscious, as well as unconscious, functions are included in his definition. The psyche consists of two complementary areas, conscious and unconscious, whose characteristics polarize, like male/female. The ego, which is the focus of consciousness, can move—more or less—into either area.

Each of us make contact with the world and adjust to its demands in a unique way. But Jung, after a long and careful investigation, concluded that the psyche had four distinct ways of working. In each individual, one of these ways was habitual and conscious, while the other three were largely unused and, for the most part, unconscious. He called these four ways of working "the four functions" and labeled them thinking, feeling, sensation and intuition. A person may be any one of these types, depending on which function he or she normally uses. If we were perfectly balanced people, we could consciously choose any one of the four to cope with a particular situation, but most of us would respond in one way only—the way of our "type."

The four functions are grouped into two pairs and can be imagined as being at the extremities of an equal-armed cross. Thought complements feeling, and sensation complements intuition.

The natural type is called the "dominant function," the "functional type." In figure 8, the dominant function is thought. It is the wholly conscious function, while its complement, feeling, lies wholly in the unconscious beyond the reach of the conscious will. The other two functions, you will see, are partly conscious and partly unconscious.

Another functional type—say sensation—would have that function at the top, in the conscious world, while its complement, intuition, would lie at the bottom of the diagram completely in

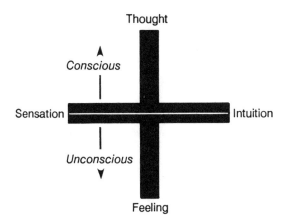

Figure 8. Jung's four functions.

the unconscious. The other two functions—thought and feeling—would be part conscious and part unconscious.

You can think of your unconscious function as the "inner you"; its characteristics determine your *inner attitude,* just as your conscious function determines the *outer attitude*—the face you show to the world. Ideally each of the four functions should be capable of being used as required. Such a degree of wholeness is rare; it is one of the goals of occult training.

Here are the basic characteristics of the four functional types. Which one are you?

> *Thinking Type:* Understands things and adjusts to the world by logical thinking, by deductions. The criterion is "true" or "false."

> *Feeling Type:* Understands things in terms of emotions. Here the criteria are "pleasant" or "unpleasant," "agreeable" or "disagreeable."

> *Sensation Type:* This is an irrational function, that is, it does not involve judgment, but perceives without evaluation. The sensation type registers the world about it as stimuli of one sort or another, rather than interpreting it in terms of feeling or thought.

> *Intuition Type:* This also is an irrational function. Like sensation, it "perceives," but in this case by an unconscious means which embraces the inner meaning of things.

It is notoriously difficult to see yourself clearly, so it may be better to get a friend to tell you what type he or she thinks you are. It is interesting to try to work out how you would react to a given situation in your life using your unconscious function rather than the usual conscious one; it can be a real eye-opener.

The symbolism of Malkuth on the Tree of Life has the four alchemical elements ascribed to it. Earth, air, fire and water are simply different conditions of energy—or different conditions of matter if you prefer to call it that. Air is the subtlest and most free-moving and earth is the densest. It is interesting to compare the four psychological types with the elements:

Earth:	Sensation type
Air:	Intuitive type
Fire:	Thinking type
Water:	Feeling type

One of the aims of the Jungian system of psychology is the integration of the unconscious functions of the soul with the conscious content. If this is done in a properly controlled manner, all sorts of valuable faculties, attitudes and enthusiasms are made consciously available for use. It is interesting that the earlier work of the Western Occult Tradition aims at similar results, although it uses different jargon.

The Jungian system lays great stress on the idea of "opposites," although possibly a better word would be "complementaries." The theory is that the soul is arranged like an electric battery, with two poles, one negative and the other positive. The difference between them makes the system work. Conscious and unconscious are the two great complementaries and there is a constant flow of energy between them, as in our picture of a battery.

Now the vast inner world of the soul—which is six-sevenths of the whole person—divides itself into two parts. The first part contains "forgotten" material together with things we do not want to face up to. This area is called *the personal unconscious*. The second part is a broader and deeper area which contains the fundamental drives common to all mankind. This area is known as *the collective unconscious*. Jung also noted another, even deeper, part which he considered could never be made conscious.

You will remember that we divided up the inner world in a threefold manner when considering humanity from an evolutionary viewpoint. Now we are in a position to compare these two classifications:

Personality	Conscious
	Personal unconscious
Individuality	Collective unconscious
Spirit	That part of the unconscious that can never be made conscious

On the Tree, consciousness could be represented by the sephirah Malkuth; the personal unconscious, by the triangle Net-zach-Hod-Yesod; the collective unconscious, by the next higher triangle of Chesed-Geburah-Tiphareth; and that part of the unconscious that can never be made conscious, by the supernal triangle Kether-Chokmah-Binah. In this use of the Tree, Mal-kuth signifies not only the brain but also the conscious part of the soul.

If the comparisons we have made are accepted as a rough guide, you will see that the various non-physical bodies of each person are composed of the "material" of the unconscious world. The kingdom of heaven is, indeed, within—so is hell!

If you consider the abstract mind (look it up on the charts), you will see that it is deep in the unconscious. To get to it, you have to make a journey through the unconscious realms. So before this level of consciousness is available to you all the time, a lot of work has to be done. Much of the unconscious needs to be made conscious, a lot of buried material brought up into the light and a number of twists and blockages removed.

To reach the goal, the "paths must be made straight," as the bible says. First the conscious mind is strengthened and trained; then the unconscious depths are slowly opened up and a "Jacob's ladder" constructed between inner and outer levels. One reason that ritual is so widely used in the Western Occult Tradition is that it speaks the language of the unconscious worlds. By its means, the unconscious can be safely aligned with the conscious self, under the control of the spirit.

The stages in the practical work devoted to this work are known as the Lesser Mysteries, and no student should be allowed to leave this stage until a reasonable degree of integration is attained. As the work of the next stage, the Greater Mysteries, is concerned with the individuality, you will see that the preliminary work, though it may be long and painful, cannot be avoided. The preparatory work of building the road to the gates of the true Self is vital; no one can build on shifting sand. The great psychological system of Jung will be considered later in more detail.

CHAPTER EIGHT

Esoteric Physiology

THIS CHAPTER IS about the make-up of the human being. Here we are not concerned with the flesh and bones of natural humanity. Glorious though the human animal is, esoteric physiology regards the physical form as merely the vehicle for the manifestation of the love, wisdom and power of the inner being who is eternal, indestructible, and timeless. So we shall spend a little time considering the essential (inner) constitution of the human being—you and me.

Various special terms are used to define the different levels of a human being. Unfortunately, some of these definitions are frequently used loosely. For this reason, it will be necessary to spend a little time in revising our terms of reference.

The Individuality

The personality is the vehicle of an incarnation. Through it contact is made with what most people call "the real world." Through it impressions are gained and experience on this plane is amassed. The individuality is the vehicle of an evolution—a vast span of time. The individuality makes its will known through its personalities and stores the essence of their experience. The spirit is eternal. It seeks the furtherance of the plan and works through the individuality.

At the end of a complete evolution, all manifestation is withdrawn into the "Secret Heart of God." As above, so below; the individuality is likewise withdrawn into the "secret heart" of the spirit, which absorbs the essence of its aeonial experience. In the next evolution, a new individuality will evolve on the basis of the spirit's experience to date. And so the process will continue until the spirit transcends the limitation of this system and becomes as a god. However, godhood is some way off for most of us, so let us return to matters nearer home.

It will be obvious by now that the individuality stands in much the same relationship to the current personality as does spirit to the individuality. As the individuality guides its personality, so does the spirit guide its individuality toward the areas of experience best suited to its experience.

The personality, nevertheless, is the *only* means of gaining direct experience of the physical world, and the aim of evolution is to bring the kingdom down to earth. So it must be obvious that there is a pressing need to straighten out the kinks and twists in the personality so it becomes a better vehicle for action and perception in the world.

After a certain degree of evolution, the individuality becomes capable of producing personalities that have at least some awareness of its needs. The process is then cumulative. As it evolves, each new personality can express more of the true purpose of its individuality. Thus the individuality evolves faster, can produce even better personalities, and so on. If you feel a yearning for the invisible realities, in whatever form, then you may well be at this point yourself.

The individuality does not, of course, act entirely of its own volition; it is a vehicle of the spirit—acting and reacting to the conditions of the "higher" non-physical planes. However, this ancient storehouse of energy, knowledge, and experience within each one of us is so vast compared with the personality that it may often *appear* to function as a separate being.

Ideally, the personality should operate as a true child of its parent, the individuality, on the planes of dense matter. Unfortunately, due to mistakes in the past, the projection is invariably a poor copy of its originator. Thus there is a "split" between the two levels; communication is seriously affected and the personality may have developed different, and sometimes opposing, motives. Problems of this sort are the rule.

Now let us imagine a perfect situation: no split. The personality would interpret the wishes of the individuality in terms of the physical plane; it would select the best method and act accordingly. But until that happy day, the greater self has to impress its will upon its lower vehicle less directly. Dreams are one example of the working of the individuality reflected into and expressed in the language of the personal unconscious. Many dreams appear to be no more than randomly selected episodes from the day's events. But others seem to have deep meaning, although the significance may not always be clear. However, all dreams repay examination. The point is not so much the apparently trivial nature of some of the events but how they are arranged and what they mean to the personality.

Think of the individuality as someone with an urgent need to communicate his wishes. But there is a language barrier and he is forced to convey his needs by using photographs torn out of the daily newspaper. He has no choice but to use the best pictures he has at hand!

Due to the splits mentioned before, the personality has developed a consciousness and identity of its own. This is derived from its experiences of the world about it—the criteria of pleasure and pain, life and death, loss and gain, safe and dangerous, and ideas of morality—all colored by its psychological type, mentioned in the last chapter. Thus, any communication received directly from "above" would probably be denied access to consciousness anyway because it was unacceptable in some way. Dreams avoid this critical mechanism of the mind and can act as valuable messengers. But it is a sorry situation—rather like the general controlling an army in the field being restricted to giving instructions to his troops by means of a series of charades, to which they give only an occasional glance. The results are best not even imagined! This is the situation which exists within the soul of the average intelligent and cultured person in the Western world today. This is also the situation a psychiatrist has to deal with in dream analysis. And unless you are already an adept, this includes you.

While dreams can certainly guide the personality and greatly affect the pattern of life, other methods are used increasingly by the individuality as you evolve. Intuitional thinking is one of these, and can take the form of anything from a "hunch" to a complete idea which could take many words to express. Such impressions often appear to arise in the mind spontaneously, being transmitted when the personality is otherwise engaged and thus off-guard.

One of the results of occult training should be to increase this way of working. The training is simple, though by no means easy. The mind, which is often the chief offender, has to be trained to take orders rather than give them all the time. The mental and emotional blockages and twists have to be removed with psychological help. Students must gain some idea of who and what they are, rather than what they think they are. The aim is to get the personality to the point where it resembles its creator, the individuality. Then, and only then, can effective communication be established.

In the case of "the average person," little experience can be gained from the personality within its lifetime. The individuality must wait until death before it can absorb the experience of the lifetime. However, as we evolve, more and more data can be transmitted direct until the stage is reached when personality and individuality become, effectively, one being.

Finally, we should never forget that the individuality is made up of the substance of the inner planes, even as the personality is formed from matter of the outer planes, and the body out of dense matter. Other beings also have bodies on these levels; and the material of the planes acts as a medium for communication, as does air for the passage of sound. So, for example, the individuality can communicate via the material of its planes with other beings having bodies of the same material. Certain types of telepathy work in this way, sometimes to other individualities who have incarnating personalities, but occasionally to those who have not. Contact with Inner Plane Adepts is made in this way. The difficulty of relaying the information from such a contact to the personality still exists, however. Contact may be incomplete or distorted like an out-of-tune radio. This is yet another reason for work on the personality.

The Personality

This chapter is about physiology. Physiology is about function. In considering the functions of the personality, it is very important to avoid the error of considering it as a separate being. Some psychological systems make this mistake; Jung does not. It is vital that the personality be seen for what it is—a projection of its individuality. From the individuality its *basic structure* is determined, as are its *fundamental* attitudes and capacities.

The word "personality" comes from the Greek word *persona*, meaning a mask. It is the face you show the world, your means of coping with people and situations. Too often the personality's face conceals the true being rather than expressing it. Jung's teaching on the subject of the dominant function (which we discuss in more detail later) makes it plain that, in most of us, the "wheel of functions" is stuck in one position. That mask, which should be elastic and adaptable has, by over-specialization, achieved the opposite result. How many people do you know whose mask of "father," "sales executive," "schoolmarm," and so on, has hardened into concrete?

Body and brain are the actual instruments of the personality. The physical world is perceived through the physical senses, the brain interpreting and correlating the results. Thus the brain is really the physical instrument of the mind and links it with the sensory and motor functions. So, although the personality is certainly the furthest extension of the spirit into matter, its purpose can only be achieved by means of a body actually formed of the matter of the physical plane itself. Therefore, in the Western Occult Tradition, the physical body is never downgraded, but is given its full importance. The physical body must be nurtured, sustained, trained and loved—just as any other of our vehicles.

Earlier we mentioned the individuality's "contacts," inward to its spirit and outward to the personality; also horizontally with other intelligences on the same level. Identical principles apply to the personality. The inner contact is with its individuality and the outer, to its body-brain. But what of horizontal contacts? Let us relate this to the psychological ideas we have been discussing. Horizontal communication can be exchanged in a number of ways. First, through the dominant function (where is sited the focus of our "ordinary" consciousness). Second, exchanges can occur through the personal unconscious via the unconscious and partly conscious functions.

An example might help here. Let us consider a man or woman who is a "thinking" type. Contact could take place on the level of thought (the dominant function in this example). This is concrete-mind-to-concrete-mind communication—one of the many types of telepathy. Exchanges could also occur through the working of the unconscious function, in this example, feeling. The focus of consciousness, the thinking part, would be unaware that anything had taken place, but contact would manifest as a change in the feeling part of the self, perhaps as a change of mood, or a "gut reaction." In the case of the semiconscious functions—in this case sensation and intuition—the same sort of process would probably occur, but there might be some degree of awareness that something was happening.

The very fact that many of these contacts go unperceived by the conscious part of us does not in any way reduce their importance and their effect upon our lives. After all, the greater part of us lies in the unconscious. Psychism, telepathy and mediumship are all examples of contacts with the personality. All three of these can occur either directly, through the sort of process just mentioned, or as a result of an inward contact with the individuality.

"Psychism" could be due to the personality getting impressions through its four functions or even from the nearly physical etheric level. "Atmospheres" around people, in houses, or other highly charged spots, the seeing of ghosts, and so on, come into this category of contacts.

The personality's other sort of contact comes inwardly, through the individuality. The individuality gets the impression and the personality gives it form by choosing suitable images to express it. A cultured person might have a better stock of images than an ignorant one, so his or her psychic impression would be a more accurate representation of the original.

All occult systems lay great stress upon training students with carefully chosen symbol systems. The symbols are chosen as particularly accurate representations of the forces they symbolize. Special meditation and ritual work with these symbols equip the mind with a new alphabet to represent the subtle forces coming from within.

The word "telepathy" has been rather overworked in the past years. As we have seen, the term covers a number of quite different methods of contact. The type of telepathy featured in the famous Rhine experiments and which is still being investigated today appears to take place mostly on the level of the concrete mind. But in some cases, there seem to have been results which suggested that another method was in use. Some of the results showed prediction, for example, while in others time seemed to have slipped the other way. These effects suggest that, momentarily perhaps, the individuality was involved. There is no time on that level.

Now let us take another example of contact. Suppose an Inner Plane Adept makes a contact with you. The link will be made on the individuality level because the Adept has no vehicles working on the outer planes. So a message is transmitted to you on the individuality level which then has to pass it on to the personality *if a sufficiently clear channel between them is available.*

If the message ends up in your personal unconscious, then your unconscious function (maybe feeling) will determine the form it takes. It could be a feeling of love and exaltation coupled, perhaps, with pictures in the mind's eye. If the message gets to the concrete mind, it may come through as concrete ideas or even as words heard in the inner ear.

Now for a word about the kind of contact various spiritualist groups have practiced—mediumship. When you die, you may first feel a great sense of expansion and freedom; but otherwise you are much the same as before and "answer to the name you knew in the flesh." All you will lack is a physical and etheric body. Consequently, the laws of telepathic contact will apply to you and there are many accounts of communication between the living and the newly dead.

What is usually called a mediumistic trance is in a slightly different category of contacts than those we have been dealing with so far. Here the medium withdraws attention from the outer levels inwards. Consciousness is lost on the physical plane and concentrated upon some inner level. The communicator (you, if you were dead) then joins up with the medium's lower levels, which she has temporarily vacated. So you now have your own "higher" bodies joined up with the medium's "lower" bodies and you have a set of channels available for communication. How good these channels are depends upon the medium.

Modern occultism tends more and more to use the individuality for telepathic contact. Trance mediumship is not really suited to contact with highly evolved beings like the Inner Plane Adepts, who are, in any case, without any bodies lower than the abstract mind.

The Etheric and Physical Bodies

Finally, no appraisal of the human being could be complete without studying our physical nature, which is divided up into subtle (etheric) and dense (physical) parts. First, the etheric part—this is rather like a network or web, into whose segments the molecules of the dense physical body fit. The etheric body is the vehicle of the animal life forces, the energies which power the physical world. The "chakras," or astro-etheric energy foci, act as junctions between the inner levels and the physical body via the endocrine system. In the Eastern Occult Tradition, hatha yoga disciplines develop control over this level. The Western student is, however, strongly advised against use of these methods. The West has its own methods, suited to the rough and tumble of occidental life. Eastern techniques applied to Westerners generally reduce ability to cope with life and may produce ill-health.

The dense physical body is the furthermost outpost in the empire of spirit. If the kingdom is ever to come on earth, it will manifest in the *physical* world through *physical* bodies. This should never be forgotten. The body should be a healthy, well-coordinated animal—in the language of the alchemists of old—a "wondrous beast." Therefore, all the capacities of the body should be trained to the full. The Western Occult Tradition has little time for those who cannot work with their hands; if you cannot, then you must learn, for occultism is a craft. The grounding-point for all occult activities is the physical plane.

CHAPTER NINE

Psychology

THE PRECEDING CHAPTERS have provided a brief picture of humanity's inner structure and function. It is impossible to overstress the need to recognize two vital facts. First, that our bodies—subtle and dense—are our *only* means of action here in this world. Second, that *all* our impressions come to us through the specialized senses in our various bodies. Thus it is vital to realize, however incompletely, what we are, how we function and the nature of our relationship with the world around us.

In case you are impatient to proceed to work more specifically "occult," you should examine your understanding of the term. All true occult or magical work is aimed at bringing invisible realities into manifestation. Both the means whereby this goal is achieved and the actual doing of it are vested in the human being. You must know yourself. There are too many trance mediums whose highest sources of contact are their own complexes, and there is a surplus of self-styled magicians who can't knock a nail in a piece of wood. Not only must occultists be more sensitive than their fellows, they must be more knowledgeable and more *capable* as well. If occultism is ever to justify its boasted claim of being a science and craft, students must first treat it as such and be prepared to work accordingly.

It is particularly important that students of esoteric matters see the various divisions of their subject in perspective and within its true context. All knowledge and speculation were once assigned to one of the divisions of philosophy; the literal meaning of philosophy being "love of wisdom" (philo = love; sophia = wisdom). The disgruntled definition of a philosopher as "a blind man in a dark room looking for a black cat that isn't there," shows a fundamental misconception of the function of philosophy, for it has both a "debunking" (analytical) and a "constructive" (synoptic) aspect. Although the latter is the division most studied by students of esotericism, there is little doubt that the occult world could profit by applying some of the former as well. Debunking can do nothing but good! The main divisions of philosophy are:

1) Natural philosophy—science

2) Metaphysics—ontology, study of the real nature of existence, epistolology, the theory of knowledge, study of the problems of understanding

3) Ethics—study of the problems of human conduct

4) Logic—study of the laws of thought

5) Psychology—study of conscious and unconscious mental processes, the study of behavior

This work concentrates on two of these divisions, metaphysics—particularly the ontological aspect or the study of the true nature of existence—and psychology. In practice, certain of the psychological schools—particularly the Jungian—extend their horizons into the realms of metaphysics. This is all very right and proper as the nature of existence cannot be studied apart from humanity, for we are the "knowers" who make the study.

The Divisions of Psychology

The word "psychology" comes from the Greek "psyche"—soul, and "logos"—systematic principle. Originally psychology was a part of speculative philosophy and thus associated with metaphysics. Whereas metaphysics speculates on the soul of nature, psychology concerns itself with the individual soul and its relation to the soul of nature. However, over the past eighty years, psychology has gradually separated itself out from philosophy and developed in its own right.

The study of the subject can often bring confusion and frustration because no two schools seem to see a problem in the same way, and often give answers which are almost totally in conflict. This difficulty may be understood when it is realized that some workers are concerned with the *mechanism* of thought, while others concentrate upon the organization of thought itself; a viticulturalist would give one picture of a vintage, a wine-taster another, and a chemist yet another. There is truth in each viewpoint—but not the whole truth. The two main theoretical branches of psychology are: the propensity branch, concerned with *disposition*; the behavioral branch, concerned with *reaction*.

The first is subjectively based, and deals with behavior, instinct, personality, and the nature of the soul. The "depth psychology" of Freud, Adler, and Jung lies within this division. The second branch is objective, and deals chiefly with the physiology and anatomy of the nervous system, and is concerned with the *mechanism* of consciousness and reaction, rather than its cause.

The cyclic law operates in the field of psychological research as it does in other spheres. At first psychology was within the philosophical campus. Then, as if to gain true identity, it broke away from its parents and enjoyed a somewhat self-conscious youth.

With the schools of depth psychology, particularly the Jungian, there were signs that more maturity had brought a recognition of the wisdom of the parent philosophy. But, with the turn of the wheel, a new phase of independence has been ushered in. No doubt, in time, all will be unified. At the moment, the field is confusing, to put it mildly.

Psychotherapy—The Beginnings

When something goes wrong and an attempt is made to rectify it, knowledge is gained in the process. The stimulus provided by the need to correct an aberrant condition leads to greater depths and detail than could ever be achieved by purely academic research. Nowhere is this more true than in the field of medicine where the stimulus is human life itself. It is therefore not surprising that some of the most penetrating systems of psychology have sprung from observations of pathological mental states which often represent an exaggeration of normal human behaviors.

There have been many attempts at a comprehensive system of psychotherapy, some of considerable antiquity. However, the increase in living pressures of the last half-century have highlighted psychological problems. In the Western hemisphere an ever-increasing technological development has tended to starve the animalistic nature, on the one hand, and deny expression to spiritual values on the other. We have tended to become mind only. With the progressive influence of science has come a corresponding increase in neurosis: the unconscious is not lightly mocked.

It was Charcot (1825–1895) who first formulated in modern terms the view that disease may be due to beliefs held in the mind. Most modern men and women would accept that opinion as axiomatic, but to their Victorian forebears it was revolutionary, shocking and scandalous. H. Bernheim (1837–1919), professor of medicine at Nancy, France, became interested in the cure of certain types of illness by hypnotic suggestion. Pierre Janet (1859–1947) also investigated neurotic behavior using hypnosis. He discovered that patients under hypnosis could recall details of their lives (generally unpleasant and thus repressed) which they could not do under normal circumstances. Janet developed a technique of suggesting to the hypnotized patient that the suppressed material would be recalled under normal waking circumstances. In this way the disturbed neurotic behavior, which he believed to be the product of the "lost" memories, would be cured. This "catharsis," as Janet called it, appeared to be a successful technique.

Dissociation of consciousness appeared fundamental to many neuroses. Josef Breuer (1842–1925), a scientist of note who discovered the function of the semi-circular canals of the ear, was greatly interested in neurotic behavior. Like Janet, Breuer hypnotized his patients and encouraged them to talk, when they often recalled repressed material and reacted with strong emotions. This catharsis (Breuer used the same word as Janet, independently) appeared to bring relief.

Freud

Freud's basic thesis was founded upon two theories; the twin hypotheses of infantile sexuality and the Oedipus complex. In his early experience, Freud accepted an uncomplicated explanation of neurosis as simply the result of suppressing painful memories of actual incidents in the patient's earlier life. Later, he changed his mind after finding many cases in which no actual shock could possibly have occurred. Experience caused him to postulate two basic drives within the human psyche: the self-preservation urge and the reproductive urge. No one doubted the former, but the latter unleashed a storm. Misunderstandings occurred in both lay and scientific circles, both of whom obviously regarded the procreative drive as simply the urge to have sexual intercourse, whereas Freud meant by it a vast spectrum of "pleasure" sensations in the physical body. Thus the reproductive urge is something much more than overt sexual motivation: also it antedates the development of adult sexual activity for it begins at birth! Freud called this sexual energy "libido" and recognized infantile sucking, eating, and urination as early forms of this activity. In the adult, the drive is not limited to sexual intercourse but is commonly sublimated into expressions of emotional tenderness, forming friendships, overcoming obstacles in work, and so on.

The work on infantile sexuality for which Freud is, perhaps, best known, was developed by his co-worker and pupil Karl Abraham. Although the initial direction and impetus in this study belonged to Freud, much of the detail is due to his disciple. A brief review of the theory may be of help. The Freudian School considers the life energy (libido) as having several distinct phases. These are generally known as oral, anal, and phallic. The young baby gains pleasure from sucking and slowly becomes aware of other people. The relationship with the mother is at its basic stage. This, then is the "oral" phase.

In the two year old (or thereabouts) the focus of satisfaction passes to the anus, and toilet training presents the child with the first need for adjustment—between instinctual pleasure and the control by the mind. Immediate pleasure is sacrificed to the subtler reward of pleasing others. To some extent this phase is the pattern for all such adjustments between the demands of society and the bodily instincts. Poor adjustment in one case is very likely to compromise other such adjustments.

The phallic phase starts any time after about four years of age. Now, gratification is centered on the genital organs. It is at this time that a boy can develop feelings for his mother and ambivalent attitudes toward his father. This is the so-called Oedipus phase, of which the female equivalent is the Electra complex. Successful resolution of these sets of ideas are necessary before a proper adult emotional relationship and sexual life can develop.

From the foregoing, some idea of the practical importance of these theories may be seen. For the first ten years of his work, Freud believed in simple suppression of "real" memory as the clue to neuroses; then he came to accept the more sophisticated theory that each neurosis is the direct result of repression of libido, and that each repression causes "regression," or movement toward an earlier, infantile mode of coping with the sexual force. For example, hysteria is said to be a regression to the phallic phase, while obsession (of whatever sort) is a regression to the anal level.

In 1900 Freud wrote the first real psychology of dreams. Jung has remarked of this event that "a proper Stygian darkness had hitherto reigned over this field." Although Freud himself later modified some of his views on dream interpretation, there is no doubt that the publication of this work represented a milestone. By now, the famous Psycho-Analytic Society was in being. As a result of the cross-fertilization of argument, disagreement and discussion between the members coupled with his experience of war neuroses, Freud came to recognize that his basic theories were not equipped to deal with all the facts. So he started his great study of the structure of the personality as a whole instead of confining his attention to two of the major instincts. One of the Society's most brilliant and active members was Alfred Adler and it is largely to him that the credit must be given for convincing Freud that the ego (the conscious part of the psyche) had a notable part to play in the development of neuroses. For the first time, Freud allowed that influences not strictly "sexual" might exert profound effects on consciousness. The fruits of this study explained the individual as divided into three related but distinct systems, the ego, the super-ego, and the id. It also postulated new conditions, a life and a death instinct, and an examination of anxiety as a factor in behavior and particularly in neurosis.

Any reasonable discussion of the ego, or Freud's views on Thanatos (the death instinct), or on the important subject of anxiety, is beyond the scope of this introduction. However the relevant books are readily available. It has become a current vogue to belittle Freud and his theories. Perhaps these few lines have given enough information to show the injustice of any such denigration and may indicate a few of the great truths of the psychic world, unearthed by the one who was the founder of the depth psychology movement, and, by any standards, a great man.

Adler

Alfred Adler, born in 1870 in Vienna, was the first of the original group of depth psychologists to break away from the idea that unconscious forces were the chief motivators in human behavior. In Freud's system, the instinct is a source of psychic energy; but Adler's developing psychology stressed the *environment* with its concomitant *social pressures* as the main influence in human life. In Freud's system, these aspects and their reactive element in the human psyche—the will to power—occupied, in Jung's words, "a poky little corner in his psychology." For Adler this "ego instinct" occupied a central position.

In the Adlerian thesis, libido is based upon the "will-to-power"—the philosophy of Nietzsche. Every individual has some characteristic of inferiority which he or she compensates by developing unconsciously a complementary "life-pattern." Adler maintained that there are three basic responses of inferiority: normal compensation; retreat into futility; neurotic over-compensation. Adler's School regards disease as primarily a "protest against conditions of inferiority" even though there may be an obvious physical cause as well. Healthy people have "realistic and social goals," neurotics have "unreal and egocentric goals."

In his study of psycho-pathology, Adler attached a great deal of importance to the relationship of parents to the children, the order of birth, whether only children, etc. He tended to play down the idea of the unconscious and the theory of repression. Although often scorned as superficial by orthodox Freudians, Adler emphasized the vital role of social contact in both normal and pathological personalities.

Jung

Carl Gustav Jung was born in 1875 in Basel, Switzerland. He died in 1961 at the age of eighty-five, having created a great psychological system. Morrish has said of Jung that he "has approached nearer the ultimate Ancient Wisdom . . . than any other Western psychologist." He was a man with an extraordinary breadth of interest. By the more orthodox of his fellow psychologists he was often regarded as a learned eccentric who dabbled in metaphysics. But workers in other fields as far apart as physics and zoology have found his profundity and insight "more meaningful than the offerings of academic psychologists." His critics might have found his theories more easy to refute had he not been such a brilliant (and obviously successful!) psychiatrist. It might be said that a man of Jung's stature would have succeeded no matter what system he followed. This is doubtful but, even were it true, it demonstrates the undisputed competence of the man—even in his critic's eyes.

After conducting a fruitful series of experiments in mental association, he devised a number of tests designed to provide accurate pointers to unconscious activities. His findings led to a theory of "complexes," unconscious groupings of ideas with a common emotional tone. His views at that time were more or less in line with the basic Freudian thesis and he subsequently met and worked with Freud for some six years. The association finally terminated as Jung's researches drew him further apart from Freud. One fundamental point of difference was that Jung did not regard the unconscious processes as being always of an infantile or animal type. Neither did he regard them as necessarily pathological. Jung considered some of our inner strivings as a great source of growth and integration, essential for the development and flowering of the well-adjusted personality. Finally Jung broke away from the Freudian group and, after much research and a protracted self-analysis founded his School of Analytical Psychology.

The first thing that should be appreciated by any student of psychology is that the Jungian thesis cannot be adequately summarized in a few pages. Adler's "will-to-power" hypothesis can be readily understood and fairly easily condensed, but Jung's system is so all-embracing and vast in its implications—encompassing as it does religion, mythology and philosophy—that an accurate abstract is impossible. The most that can be done is to produce a framework upon which subsequent study can be based.

Jung's system is more than a psychotherapy. It aims at a complete understanding of the nature of mankind. Hence his replacement of the terms "mind" and "mental" by "psyche" and "psychic" because the former imply only consciousness, whereas the latter represent a totality of conscious and unconscious levels. By the way, the occult student should note carefully Jung's use of the term "psychic" and avoid confusion with the meaning generally attached to it in occult literature.

Possibly the most valuable of Jung's feelings, from the occult viewpoint, is his insistence on the *reality of the psyche*. He gives it equal actuality to the physical, conscious world. It has its own format and laws. Occult tradition has always taught that the laws of a plane are supreme on that plane. Therefore it is easy to agree with Jung that the psyche must be studied in the light of its own structure and laws. The vast world of the unconscious represents six-sevenths of a person; the conscious or seventh part is only the means of focusing the particular space-time system that we call the material world.

In reality, all that we experience is psychic. In his essay, "Basic Postulates of Analytical Psychology," Jung writes, "All that I experience is psychic. . . . Even physical pain is a psychic image which I experience; my sense-impressions . . . are psychic images, and these alone are the immediate objects of my consciousness . . . All our knowledge consists of the stuff of the psyche which, because it alone is immediate, is superlatively real. Here, then, is a reality to which the psychologist can appeal—namely, psychic reality."[4] From this extract alone it can be seen that Jung gives to the inner world a value and a reality equal to the outer world of effects.

Jung saw the energy of the psyche—the libido, in Freudian terms—in constant motion, with a tidal movement. The libido

---

[4]"Basic Postulates of Analytical Psychology" (1931) is included in *The Collected Works of C. G. Jung*, Vol. 8 (New York: Bollingen Foundation, 1960).

can be imagined as energy whose movement depends on a difference in polarity between two terminals. An obvious analogy would be an electric current flowing between negative and positive poles of a battery. The very existence of the current depends upon one pole's "difference" to the other. The greater the difference in potential between the terminals, the greater the energy. Without opposition of polarity, there is no movement. This psychic energy is seen to be tidal in nature, the forward motion satisfying the conscious mind's desire to work and create, while the backward (and equally important) movement satisfying the unconscious mind's desire to brood, formulate, gestate and motivate. The forward drive is toward greater adaptation to the environment, while the backward motion is concerned with adaptation to inner needs and realities.

In this description, the two poles of the circuit are seen as the conscious and unconscious aspects of the psyche, but the theory of opposites (or, more accurately, complements) applies to both nature and humanity, and was symbolized in the old Mystery Tradition temples by two pillars between which the candidate for initiation was made to stand.

Symbols

Another vital point to understand in any study of Jungian psychology is his interpretation of the word "symbol." To Jung, the word "sign" means a substitute for, or representation of, the real thing, whereas "symbol" is used in a much wider sense as something *expressing a psychic fact* that could not otherwise be formulated accurately. To take a simple example, a highway sign is a substitute for a written message. But a symbol, such as the calvary cross, expresses the totality of the psychic reality of sacrifice. Hence the universal nature of symbols as opposed to the "local" and personal nature of signs. Much of the work of esoteric groups is concerned with the construction and use of symbols.

The Ego and the Unconscious

What we call the conscious mind might be compared to the peak of a mountain rising from the sea of the unconscious. But the greater bulk of the mountain, unknown and unseen, lies beneath the water. The peak is the *ego,* the "I" that knows and wills, the focus of everyday consciousness. But many of the experiences of the conscious life are not liked, or are unacceptable socially. These memories of fear, deprivation, inferiority, rejection, lust, and so on, are ousted from consciousness by a deliberate withdrawal of attention, a refusal to face, a willed forgetting. This process is called *repression.* Repression must be carefully distinguished from *suppression,* which is merely the normal and perfectly healthy process of attention withdrawal from one subject in order to attend to others. In the case of true repression, the renegade material cannot be recalled at will, whereas suppression allows recall. Subliminal impressions, insufficiently strong to reach consciousness, are also relegated to the unconscious. The shadow land of the psyche to which all this repressed and subliminal material goes is called by Jung the *personal unconscious.* It is that part of the mountainside just beneath the unconscious waters.

The personal unconscious belongs to an individual. It is that part of the unconscious that has become personalized and populated with repressed memories and subliminal impressions. There is a fairly regular commerce between the conscious and personal unconscious. Repressed material enters the shadow world from consciousness, and there is a reciprocal flow towards consciousness which manifests in dreams, urges, irrational feelings, and actions, etc. So, compared to the vast submerged bulk of the mountain, the personal unconscious has been domesticated to some extent! Obviously, if the goal of evolution is the whole person, then material should not be repressed in the first place, but rather confronted and accepted as material for greater growth. But we do not live in a perfect world and many of the techniques of psychotherapy aim at digging up repressed matter and integrating it with the content of consciousness. Sometimes repressed material is accidently recalled by a shock or a chance association of ideas. Dreams and fantasies also carry a personal unconscious content.

Jung's earlier work on this level of the psyche revealed a peculiarity of structure whose discovery was later to play a great part in his system. His research demonstrated a tendency of ideas to become associated together around certain fundamental foci. Jung called these groups of ideas of a common type and emotional tone complexes. Some complexes are fairly superficial and may be partly conscious. Others are more basic and have their being in the personal unconscious. Others appear to exist at a far deeper level in the psyche. To these, Jung paid particular attention.

The deeper levels of the unconscious from which our consciousness emerges is called the *collective unconscious*. It is the level of the deepest drives and instincts. In it are found the very roots of the psyche and the wisdom and experience of the collective. The deepest levels are common to all humanity.

Brief mention has been made of the individuality as being a differentiation of the "substance" of the collective unconscious, just as the physical body could be defined as a differentiation of matter of the physical world. At the greatest depth of all is the spirit, which may be deduced but not defined. It is as if the spirit built up about it bodies of the various strata of the collective unconscious as it involved. If this analogy is compared with the cosmological description in Chapter 6, benefit may be gained from the study of the same theory expressed in terms of two different symbol systems. Jung himself never specifically mentions "spirit" in his works, at least not in the way that esoteric students employ the term. Nevertheless, his whole psychology implies it and there is some reason to believe that our universal nature, and the reincarnationary cycle, formed a part of his beliefs never expressed in cold print for obvious reasons. (See figure 9 on page 116.)

Archetypes

The deeper levels of the collective unconscious are common to all humanity. In our involution and evolution, it is reasonable to postulate certain common experiences for—no matter what our race, color or language—we are spiritual beings of the same type as our fellow divine sparks. These common experiences would have been fundamental to our development as human beings.

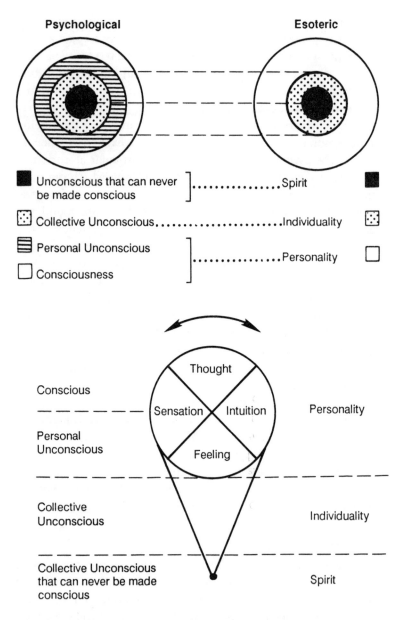

Figure 9. Psychological and occult correlations.

Such occurrences might be symbolized as the figure of the father, the mother, the virgin, the wise old man, the child, the corpse, and so on, and by such images as the sun representing the source of life, or the moon and the sea representing the hidden inner world, etc.

In the course of evolution these foci of experience built up as each attracted to itself more accumulated human knowledge of its particular type. These vast and primordial complexes of human experience Jung calls *archetypes*. It is reasonable to suppose that these primordial images were formulated during the thousands of years when the physical brain was evolving from the animal state. Archetypal symbols emerge in dream and vision— sometimes even in the semi-conscious "doodlings" on the telephone pad! While different eras and cultures may modify the form, archetypes always retain their primordial quality. Some may appear in abstract or geometrical form; others manifest as gods and goddesses, animals or plants. There is a strong mythological quality about the archetypes. In fact, it was the basic similarity between the folklore and mythology of widely different racial cultures that provided Jung with material for his investigations. Truly it can be said that had Jung not postulated the concept of the archetypes of the collective unconscious, someone else would have been forced to, if only to account for the sometimes incredible similarities of the different mythologies, let alone the similarity of dream and visionary experience the world over.

The archetypes represent the distilled essence of particularized human experience and are psychic power-houses and transformers. The basic symbol-set of an occult lodge is made up of selected archetypes.

Myths and Dreams

Jung spent a great deal of time studying myths. He maintained that although the structure of the myth is man-made and conscious, its spirit and most of its imagery come from the collective unconscious. If myths *are* the direct expression of the collective unconscious, then it is reasonable to find them in similar forms among people of all ages and races. In primitive races there is less conscious "embroidery"; therefore, the archetypal content is dominant and more easily perceived. Religion, fairy tales, poetry and some forms of drama depend for their effect on the use of archetypal imagery to evoke the greater world of the collective unconscious. That is why certain themes are guaranteed to be box-office successes.

Freud used dream interpretation as a means of accessing repressed material, but his considerations caused him to stop short at childhood experiences. While Jung also employed dreams in this way, his thinking embraced the wider sphere of the collective unconscious and the archetypes which dwell therein. His system did not limit itself to the healing of pathologies of the psyche, but extended to the healing of the whole person, to our fullest expression and the realization of our full potential.

Jung saw the dream as a spontaneous emergence of the unconscious, a "happening" out of conscious control. Herein lies the value of a dream. It is a *window* into the inner world of the psyche and repays considerable attention. Jung considered that the first step in dream interpretation was to establish the dreamer's relationship with the dream in order to interpret the significance of its symbols. A series of dreams is therefore more effective than a single one because a pattern may emerge from which the meaning of the basic symbols can more easily be deduced. There is no fixed interpretation of symbols. Black cats, when they appear, do not always indicate bad luck! The figure of a mother may mean love, warmth and comfort to one, and fear, hate, and frustration to another. Then again, there is the mother *archetype* to consider also. In other words certain symbols can be interpreted on several levels, archetypal as well as personal.

Dreams can be considered from two viewpoints—subjective and objective—they can be seen as related to the inner world or to the actual world of the physical environment. In the first case, the figures and symbols encountered represent aspects of the dreamer's inner life, while in the second they depict actual people and their relationships. In practice, a valid interpretation is sometimes possible in both ways.

Attitudinal Types

The psychologies of Freud and Adler each offer plausible explanations of neurosis. In the main, both theories are elegant systems whose validity can be verified by observation and investigation. Both theories appear to be right; both can be demonstrated as valid. But can two such opposing theories both be correct? The adherents of the two schools warred with one another; each side declaring it was right and heartily condemning its opponent. This problem gave Jung a great deal to think about. The answer he finally arrived at is typical of his genius. He saw that the approach of each of the schools was determined by its basic attitude. The Freudian looked within toward the unconscious world for its explanation, while the Adlerian looked outward toward the environment. This consideration caused Jung to wonder whether there were not two different human types, one interested in oneself and the other in the objective world. As a result of these ponderings, Jung evolved the theory of the *Attitude Type*, and postulated the two fundamental attitudes possible to a human being. These he called the *introvert* and the *extrovert*. The former looks within, and the latter, without. Properly understood, this question of two opposite types is another expression of the Law of Complementaries, the two pillars of the temple mentioned earlier. Ideally, it should be possible to use either attitude at will, but in practice each of us is predisposed toward one of the two approaches to life. The reflective nature of the introvert causes him to think before acting. Naturally, this makes him slow to act and he often has some difficulty in adapting to the outer world. Conversely, the extrovert has a positive relation to things and is attracted to them. New, unknown situations fascinate and he will jump into the unknown with both feet. Generally, the extrovert acts first and thinks afterward. However, the Law of Complementaries acts inwardly as well. An introvert has an inner attitude

of extroversion, while an extrovert has an inner attitude of intro-
version. Therefore, within every introvert there is an extrovert
trying to get out, and vice-versa!

The Four Functions

The division of the human race into two camps, extrovert and
introvert, does not cover all the differences in human personality.
The extrovert approaches the world in a particular way according
to the way in which the psyche works: likewise the introvert.
Each uses what Jung would call his or her "most developed function." Jung recognized four distinct functions. But although these
are differentiated for convenience, there will probably be very
few pure types. Chapter 7 briefly explains the arrangement of
the functions. Each functional type can be either extrovert or
introvert in approach to life, so there are eight basic types and
innumerable admixtures. A thinking type could be pure or mixed
with sensation or intuition in any degree. The thinking type
could not, however, be mixed with feeling: the two are complementaries so feeling is the unconscious attitude. The same principle applies to any of the other functional types. A few examples
may clarify the picture, but the possible combinations are almost
endless. After all, human beings are individuals.

The Extroverted Thinking Types direct themselves toward the
outer world. Interested in "facts," if they concern themselves with
ideas at all, ideas will arise from the facts of what they call
"reality." They are down-to-earth, cannot see beyond fact, and
thus limit themselves.

The Introverted Thinking Types are chiefly concerned with
ideas, not facts. They are theorizers, "creative" thinkers. They
are interested in the inner world. They may be shy and withdrawn
and give little attention to others or to the world about them.

The Extroverted Feeling Types are generally well adjusted to
the world, and always seem to "fall on their feet," being much

concerned with personal relationships. Often possessing tact and charm, these people make social life possible. Better examples display a genuine desire to help those less fortunate, while the worst may be insincere, artificial or flamboyant.

The Introverted Feeling Types often seem very different from the extrovert. Often appearing withdrawn and reserved, their deep sympathy and understanding emerge only within the shelter of a family group or with close friends. This type may express the inner feelings in art or religion. They are valuable close friends.

The Extroverted Sensation Types take everything exactly as it comes. There is little or no imagination and no attempt to use thought for analysis of impressions. Arousing sensation is the principal aim of this type, and they may display calm and apparently reasonable natures. Often fun-loving and jolly, their goal is seeking things to give them pleasure and they are often concerned with arousing sensations in others. The worst are thrill-seeking hedonists.

The Introverted Sensation Types are often overwhelmed by sensory impressions. They are difficult to understand and ever concerned with inner images. *Experiencing* sensation is an aim of this type, but the sensation may arise from inner stimuli; the objective world is a secondary consideration. Such people often have vivid imaginations, see "castles in the air" and have curious psychic experiences. Musicians and artists can be found in this type.

The Extroverted Intuitive Types generally dislike all established "safe" things. They follow inner perception and can be ruthless with others when in pursuit of inner goals. They rarely reap the benefit of their actions for they constantly chase possibilities rather than actualities. They rarely complete an activity beyond the point when they think the goal is in sight. Personal life is frequently chaotic, but rarely boring!

The Introverted Intuitive Types are often mystical dreamers and seers, or unfortunately, cranks. Certain of the prophets were, no doubt, of this type, but it is easy to see how the pursuit of perception can degenerate into obsession with the perception itself rather than with the uses to which it might be put. Blake is often quoted as a good example of this type—he was both poet and artist.

Religion and the Individuation Process

Jung was unique among psychologists in having postulated a *religious instinct.* He considered adoration and the urge toward unity with the divine as natural as any of the other basic drives of mankind, and said that psychic health and stability depended on the proper expression of this. Surely, religion's prime aim should be to unite the inner and outer worlds in order to bring the kingdom of heaven to earth. While Jungian psychology aims at unity of the inner and outer worlds in the individual, one thing is certain—until individual unity is achieved, no world harmony is possible. Individuation is the term he used to describe this process of unification, which he saw as the progressive development of the whole person. It is a process of integration whereby the unconscious urges are recognized, reconciled, and consciously expressed in attitude and action. This is a profoundly "religious" operation, whether one thinks in terms of energies and forces in the unconscious or in more conventional mystical symbolism. The aim is the same—perfection.

Those stages of the Western traditions known as the Lesser Mysteries also aim at achieving a reasonable measure of individuation, and the stimulation of the inner nature aided by the forces of initiation.

CHAPTER TEN

Karma and Destiny

IN EARLIER CHAPTERS we mentioned errors and abuses of free will when discussing evolution. Now we need to consider these rather vague terms in more detail because they have an immediate practical effect on everyone who reads this book. First let us define our terms.

We mentioned karma once before. Karma is a word borrowed from Eastern occultism. In practice it means "cause and effect." Destiny means a part of the great plan for which a particular human being is responsible. You have your part; I have mine. Each part is a tiny jewel in a vast mosaic; each part is unique; each part is vital. To see how karma and destiny work together we must consider karma in more detail.

Karma is based on the idea that every action generates a reaction. A pendulum set in motion continues to move until its forces get into balance. The universe is a closed system and any displaced force has to be balanced by its opposite. We are more than just physical beings: we can "act" emotionally by feeling, and mentally by thinking. Likewise the reactions to our actions can be on non-physical levels as well.

In practice, karma is the gathering of the fruits of past actions. This is the way it works: imagine the plan held in the Mind of God as a network of forces within which we have freedom to express ourselves individually and so make unique contribu-tions to the plan. If we align with these forces in our work, then the only reactions are movements which help us forward on our true path and which support our efforts. Such people would be said to be working out their destiny.

But if, due to wrong ideas about destiny, we try to act against the forces of the plan, then these forces oppose us to the degree of our misalignment. This reaction is experienced as "karma." This is more a matter of physics than of ethics. If we think of karma simply as a reaction, then it could be "good" as well as "bad." However, in the West we tend to restrict the use of the word to the unfortunate results of wrong (misaligned) actions.

Of course the obvious question is "why"? Why should we deliberately act in opposition to forces which are helpful to us? The answer lies in the mystery of free will. Free will seems to be the great experiment in this universe: a novel idea in universe-building: a Great Entity, God, cooperating with a vast swarm of lesser beings of the same type. Both have free will. Both have responsibilities. God embodies His experience in a perfect ab-stract form and maintains it. We have to fill in the details. We are each responsible for one facet in a uniquely individual way, finally expressing our creativity on the densest possible level of being. Both God and people are the creators.

Now many occultists believe that, before we entered the scheme, there were other beings involved: beings who had reached a relative perfection and who were all completely aligned with God's purpose. These beings assisted in the building of the framework of the universe. Senior in evolution to us, some of these Lords of Flame, Form, and Mind as they are often called, later became known as the archangels "who stand in the presence of God."

So, according to this theory, we had a well-organized structure already waiting when the time came for us to do our work. But, whereas our predecessors were attuned to the plan, we were not. We had to adapt our creativity to the purposes of our destiny. Tradition declares that this is where the trouble started. Many reacted against the plan, preferring to play other parts than their agreed role in the vast scheme. Some reacted against working within the limitations of dense matter. Others reacted against their companions. All are said to have reacted somehow.

The spirit, the nucleus of any man or woman, contains both female and male in perfect balance. Yet on the physical level of the plan, animal bodies had to be used to work within the dense constriction of matter. These animal forms were either male or female. And to work out our part of the plan in dense substance, a body of a particular sex was needed. One spirit's destiny in matter might demand a female body; another's, a male. But in all cases, the balanced perfection had to be abandoned for a one-sided expression. Often there was a reluctance to accept the required sexual role.

Enough has probably been said to indicate the many ways in which uncontrolled free will causes misalignment with the great forces which maintain the structure of the universe. Misalignment means karma. Yet the destructive possibilities of free will must have been known to the Mind of God.

Evolution could be likened to a vast canvas on which a supreme Master has painted the outlines of a form of indescribable beauty. And on which a horde of selfish, irresponsible, squabbling children are daubing paint apparently at random. Yet somehow the outlines shine through. Imagine the sorrow of the artist who knows what the final masterpiece should be, yet who cannot, by his own free choice, intervene. Aeons must pass as the children grow to learn the lessons of discipline and cooperation and eventually come to realize their parts in the creation of the masterpiece. Such is evolution in a universe whose keynote is free will. We are assured that the results will be worth the pain. Having eaten of the fruits of the Tree we will become as gods, knowing good and evil.

You will probably see that all our troubles are the results of karma because you are *what* you are because of your karma. You are *where* you are because of your karma. And, your future depends upon your past and upon your actions *now.* You are actually creating your future at this moment.

What can you do about karma? Before any sort of answer can be given we shall have to look at some more data. Perhaps you have wondered how we could oppose the forces of the plan in the first place. After all, we seem to be insignificant beings compared with the immensity of the universe. But we are not insignificant. This is a reality all students of occultism should clearly realize.

We are of the same nature as God and are immensely powerful beings in our own right. So it was (and is) possible for us to oppose our own destiny. Of course, if we swim against the tide we use up energy—even to stay in one place. So one of the effects of karma is to tie up a lot of energy in maintaining false positions; so our power as creative beings is greatly reduced. As long as we continue in the wrong direction, we are crippled.

We have been divided against ourselves and our God since the dawn of time. But there is some light in the darkness. The power of the spirit is not limited by time or space. And even false destiny contains something of the true plan. The teachings of occultism provide a path between karma and destiny. However, anyone who has tried to give up smoking knows that to break a deep-seated habit is not easy. It is painful. It takes guts. But who wants to remain a half-being?

Karma and Life

If we follow our destiny, we ought to be powerful, happy, peaceful, creative, healthy and bursting with enthusiasm and life. Generally, we are few of these things. Karma is the cause. How do we change?

Some think they must first get themselves perfected before they can be of service to others. This is a mistake. Each karmic knot untied releases a little more of destiny. Every wrong pattern of living corrected liberates its quota of energy. These things affect the world profoundly—especially when done with deliberate intention.

Some students apply themselves to the task of getting straightened out with grim determination and ruthless efficiency. The determination and efficiency are welcome; the attitude is not. Regeneration is a word we use to describe this process of correcting past mistakes. It means making a new person of yourself, so don't treat the rectification of past mistakes as a boring, dreary chore. Don't get obsessed with your own sinful unworthiness. If you tackle it correctly, regeneration can give you a new experience a day. Think of it as a journey of exploration complete with surprises, hard work, difficulties, dangers and fulfillment. Coming to grips with karma is exactly like an expedition into an unknown land. It demands the same qualities, probably the most important of which is a sense of humor!

This lack of humor often causes budding occultists to deny themselves the fruits of their successes. If you put something right in yourself, then by all means thank God on bended knee. But afterwards find some way of *using* your new freedom. Get some fun out of regeneration: *enjoy* it! Then make sure other people benefit too.

Karma is a matter of wrong inner attitudes that have become ways of life, it is dynamic. It is not a "sin" or several sins, but a whole set of attitudes. And from attitudes come ways of life. Karma causes problems ranging from impotence to world war. Ways of life make patterns and, when these habit tracks are examined by someone who knows what to look for, it is possible to see both karma and destiny. A "karmic" attitude makes an appropriate form; a "destiny" attitude also makes form. What are these forms? For a start, body, environment, relationships and job all reflect karma. They represent our inner state. We are totally responsible for them, but we can also change them.

How? First by getting to know yourself and facing up to what you are and are not. Then, by examining your environment and relationships, finding areas that need changing and doing something about them; and going on acting until the change is complete. Then moving on to another trouble spot, and so on.

Simple? Certainly. But by no means easy. The big "occult secret" in all of this lies in *attitude*. Normally, evolution works unconsciously and slowly, correcting errors and removing blockages like water wearing away a stone. Occultists take control of their own evolution *consciously*. The keyword is "consciously."

Coming to Grips with Karma

In theory it should be possible for you to sit down, do a little self-analysis, make a mental list of your errors and shortcomings, work out the basic cause, change the inner attitude, and then act accordingly: in theory, that is! In practice it just isn't possible to work like that. You are not just dealing with an erroneous idea or two, but wrong habits that have changed the very nature of your being, wrong actions that have incurred debts and responsibilities. Possibly a very high grade adept could do it. But then, an adept would not need to.

Where do you start? What do you do? When? You start NOW. Where you start does not really matter much. It isn't where you start, but *how* that matters. What you do is determined by what you are. There is no need for a psychic investigation into past lives; you have all the evidence you need in your present life and it's all around you.

So you start on the physical plane. You take a small area of your life—any small area of your life—in which there are difficulties and there, in that area, establish *order* and *control*. And, having established the control of your true will in that area, then *maintain it*. It must be maintained. Do not just philosophize—do something. Do not think—act.

The procedure is very simple but there can be difficulties. Most people are too ambitious. Having chosen the part of their life they want to correct, they rush in and start "correcting" everything in sight. After a while the situation overwhelms them, interest is lost and the previous condition re-asserts itself. Another non-success has been added to the list and the habit of failure has been reinforced. Keep in mind the occult precept called the Law of Limitation. It says that if you want to get anything done in this universe, then you have to limit yourself. Steam escapes from an open vessel; but confine it in a boiler and you have the ingredients for an industrial revolution. That is how the last one started. You must confine your urge toward regeneration as the steam was confined in the boiler. You restrict it in two dimensions—space and time. Instead of diffusing your efforts, you confine them to a limited and very specific area and time of your life. You say, "I will do something about *this, daily* for *two weeks* and then re-examine the problem." That is all you have to do. If continued, the method is a certain success. When you reduce one area of your life to order *and maintain it,* you can consider extending your control.

Opposition to your enterprise is certain; most of it will come from within. The mind, programmed by the basic error, will invent a host of reasons for not continuing the project. It may be made to appear ridiculous, pointless, time-wasting, futile, unrealistic, and so on. The emotions will probably get involved too. You may experience feelings of boredom, anger, irritation and other reactions. All these are good signs and show that your work is effective. If you look at your reactions in as detached a way as you can, you may learn something new about yourself. In time, your reactions may fall into well-defined patterns. If you examine these with detached sympathy you may be able to get some ideas about the basic error you made ages ago when you decided in some way and to some degree to "go it alone."

At this point the problem may have been corrected on the physical level; you may have produced order and control, but the originating cause—which is really the mental attitude—remains. That is why reactions occur, the mind is trying to re-establish the old pattern while you (the real you) are busy establishing a new way of life. From this description you may be able to discern the true value of this apparently trivial exercise. In the average person, wrong attitudes and errors have produced a "false will." Occasionally—particularly in moments of stress—the true will operates, but generally the false will rules. As soon as you *consciously* try to change the patterns and work from the physical plane, then the old habits are broken and, for a time, the true Self is in the saddle. A new line of command is set up: true will, mental idea, emotional drive and physical action. Be it ever so humble, a real spiritual impulse has been conceived, executed and grounded in earth.

As the practice continues, the new system of management gets more firmly established and new habit-patterns are set up. Of all the benefits obtained, the most important accomplishment is getting yourself back in charge. So, when you struggle to maintain order in some small aspect of your life using this method, remember—you are planning a coup, you are putting yourself back on the throne.

It doesn't matter where you start—any area of your life will do—but people often feel the need for some help when starting an enterprise with such far-reaching effects. Table 5 shows you some life areas that may help you decide which karmic pattern you want to work on first. It presents five general areas in life and breaks them down into the regions which seem to contain most of our fears, sorrows and frustrations. There are many more. In general you may find it more useful to select an area dealing with the physical world, at least at first. Do not forget to limit your project in size and time. Here are two examples taken from life.

Example 1: John Smith

John is fifty years old, married twenty-five years, balding on top, slow in his movements, discontented in expression, employed as a minor executive in an insurance company. He never made the higher grades. His job bores him. He lives in an apartment in the city with his wife; he likes her well enough, but the marriage seems to have been flat for the last ten years. He has no hobbies

Table 5. Karmic Life Areas

Personal	Money/Resources	Home	Relationships	Job/Career
Health	Enough?	General condition Upkeep Appearance	Marriage	Fulfillment
Appearance	Proper management		Physical relationships including stability, sex, communication, friendship, companionship, shared interests, pleasure, trust, resources (money, possessions), mutual help	Money
Clothing	Right spending	Cleanliness	Friendships, including communication, trust, shared interests, mutual help	Right location
Habits	Right saving Right investment	Order Comfort Beauty		Stability Prospects Relationship with others

except occasional reading. A typical evening would include a tray
meal (but he likes his food), television, perhaps a little reading.
He feels he has missed out on life and the world has gone sour on
him. Once interested in spiritualism, he met too many cranks
and became disillusioned.

One lunchtime, listening to someone talk about the occult
in lurid terms, he experienced a strong reaction, "He's talking
nonsense—it's not like that." The reaction died down, but
throughout the afternoon he had occasional fleeting twinges of
excitement. On the way home, he called in at a bookshop to get
the latest thriller. While browsing, he came upon this book, and
bought it on an impulse. He read it through dinner, T.V. and
his wife's occasional comments. He read this chapter (and was
startled to find an example just like him!) and, at 2 A.M. next
morning went to sleep determined to do something about himself.
His last thoughts were that this was the first excitement he had
felt in twenty years.

Next day was Saturday. Normally he slept in. But this morning he woke early with a feeling that he had something to do.
For a few moments he had an argument with himself—this was
Saturday and he should be sleeping. But he remembered the
words in the book, "Don't think—ACT." So he stumbled out of
bed quietly, for he did not want his wife to wake. He did not
want to get caught doing something that might seem foolish.
Would she think it foolish? He could not decide. He realized that
he did not know what his wife thought. He paddled to the kitchen
via the bathroom and caught sight of himself in the glass. The
reflection looked back at him, untidy, grey-faced, paunchy. He
put the coffee on and went to get the book and read the chapter
again over his coffee. Which life-area to choose was a problem.
Work was hell, but he did not think much of his home either.
Then the picture of himself in the bathroom glass rose up before
him and he made his decision. He had not felt really healthy for
years; sometimes he felt lousy. John chose to work on his health
first.

What to do next? He considered diet, calisthenics, jogging and weight-lifting. He had been fit once and had played football in the Army. What had happened to him since? At that point he made up his mind, he would get checked-out medically. It was Saturday so he would have to wait to make an appointment. "Sometime next week," he thought, "when I get some time." But the book said "use the discipline of time," so he determined to telephone from the office on Monday morning. Somehow there was a feeling of disappointment in this. He wanted to do something now.

At this point his meditation was interrupted by the arrival of his wife who wanted to know why he could not sleep. John countered by saying he was a bit low and had thought about getting a check-up next week sometime. To his surprise, she agreed that he needed one and confided that she felt the same. Over breakfast they talked about the early days of their marriage. They had not talked as much for years. The weekend passed normally enough except that several times John got a furtive feeling of excitement which vanished when he tried to think what it could mean.

Monday morning came as it always does, but he was up earlier than usual. On Sunday he found a diary he had been given at Christmas. This was to be a record of his project. He took it to work with him and, under the bold heading PROJECT APOLLO, he recorded the time of his doctor's appointment.

When it came to it, the visit was rather an anti-climax. There was nothing really wrong with him that a sensible diet and regular exercise would not cure. He would have to lose some weight. He and his wife talked about it when he got home. It seemed that his wife had had some dietician's training at college and diets were discussed at length. After dinner, the talk continued with John debating what form his exercise should take. Remembering a book he had once read, yoga was suggested. To his surprise, the idea was received with enthusiasm. She had seen a series on T.V., "not the breathing and funny stuff, just the exercises." He decided to enroll in classes at the local sports center. But by now he was aware of his tendency to let things drift, so he made a note in his project diary to enroll tomorrow after work.

Next day turned out to be one hell of a day. John was exhausted and strongly tempted to let things ride for a while. But the thought of his entry in the diary, not to speak of his wife's questions, persuaded him that the effort had to be made. He drove wearily to the center. By the time he arrived, Project Apollo, special diet and yoga seemed ridiculous. He wanted nothing more than to sit down and watch T.V. But he was there now and might as well do something. His luck was in. There was a free place on the course starting on Friday. Quite suddenly the tiredness and depression lifted, and he got the feeling he was moving at last and that there was something deep inside him trying to get up and go.

The week passed slowly. Salad lunches and balanced evening meals became the rule. Meanwhile, John fretted for action. His normal routine was broken and there seemed to be nothing to put in its place. He took to day dreaming. Sometimes he fantasized scenarios involving his colleagues at the office. Occasionally the scenes were violent. Often he brooded upon the past and what he might have made of it. He did his work well enough. The restless energy that now filled him consumed his daily quota of boring tasks in half the time, which gave him more opportunity to brood. He was accustomed to being the target of office jokes but now he reacted with anger. The excitement of his original discovery had left him. Now he was simply angry and resentful.

Friday arrived. John felt he had been through a battle; his fellow workers felt the effects too; a new aspect of John had been revealed. Once again, he battled to the center. Traffic was worse than usual. He was late and found the class already assembled.

Feeling foolish, fat, and fifty, he listened sullenly to the introductory talk. When it came to doing the initial exercises, there was worse to come. A strange garment was produced and he was expected to wear it for the classes and the exercises at home. He felt worse than ever; one and a half hours gone—and for what? His stomach protested, he had a headache, he was tired, and he looked ridiculous. But to have left would have made him look an even bigger fool.

They sat on mats and attempted to follow the apparently effortless postures of the instructor. But John soon realized that he was not alone in his difficulties. Others looked, he thought, even worse than he and some could not manage even the simplest exercise. He redoubled his efforts and was rewarded by a word of approbation from the instructor.

Suddenly, he felt good. His stomach protested still, his head still troubled him, he was more tired than ever, and he now ached all over! But he no longer cared whether he looked ridiculous or not, and he felt good.

The lesson ended, John eased his aching body into his car and drove home. On the way, he debated how much to tell his wife. He guarded his new-found interest jealously, and was reluctant to disclose how good he felt about it. But to his surprise, his wife was sympathetic, full of questions and constructive ideas.

As he sank his protesting limbs into a hot bath, he found himself wanting to talk and share his feelings about the past week's purgatory and tonight's experiences. They talked over supper and into the night. He felt he knew her better than ever before and experienced a spasm of rage at the wasted years.

The months went by. The yoga was endured and finally, enjoyed. Diet was more difficult but he kept at it. He felt better, looked better, and dressed better. But his emotional life was in chaos. Sudden bouts of anger, impatience, jealousy, resentment, and a strange nostalgia chased across his consciousness, apparently at random. He, whose life had been a model of regular, well-ordered thoughts and feelings, now felt himself to be on a battlefield. But he was alive at last and, amid all the confusion, he knew it.

As time passed, it became increasingly apparent that his real problems were centered around his wife and his feelings for her. As his physical problems diminished, his emotional life rose up crying for justice. Slowly he realized he had retreated into well-ordered futility in order to escape from problems he could not confront. During his yoga session one morning it came to him that his problems and his needs were all centered around one theme—relationship. So John, a dull, sluggish man with a health problem, is now well and active but torn with wild feelings; a man with an emotional problem.

The inner path was entered through a mundane door, a health problem. The start was humdrum, the way obstructed by boredom, inertia, embarrassment, fatigue and reluctance. Yet it led him to a set of realizations that were like a little re-birth; and a re-birth always involves a re-orientation. The pursuit of health led to a confrontation with a hitherto unrecognized problem. That problem is likely to be central to John's karma: and if it is not itself fundamental, it will inexorably lead to something that *is*. In treading the by-roads leading to that central error, he will become a new man.

The ingredients of success are thought, choice, action and perseverance, all contained within a disciplined framework of time. Reading about it is only the start. Try it, and keep on trying it and you will never be the same again.

• • •

We have looked at the case of John Smith in some detail in order to show one example of how this approach to the problems of karma can work out. John Smith was an ordinary man in an ordinary situation. No occult fireworks were involved, just an intensification of life. Occultism, properly applied, does just that—it speeds up evolution. But remember that John's struggles and ultimate progress were based upon fundamental occult hypotheses, karma, destiny and the Law of Limitation. Our second example can be dealt with in less detail.

Example 2: Belinda Jones

Belinda has a trim figure, is well dressed, attractive, and conscious of her appearance. Recently divorced, she lives alone in a small apartment maintained in perfect order. Like John, she became interested in the occult. In her case, the trauma of divorce provided the occasion. She too read this book and decided that something had to be done because life was not tolerable any more.

Belinda had entered into a series of relationships before her marriage, all of them unsatisfactory in some way, all of them ending painfully. Marriage was to have been the answer. Permanence and stability were surely the solution to her problem. Yet, despite her own best efforts and those of her spouse, who was pleasant, tolerant and generous, the marriage foundered and Belinda was left with a profound and painful sense of loss and failure. Looking down the list in Table 5, "Marriage/physical relationship" was obviously the correct heading for her, but which of the subheadings applied? None of them had been really satisfactory in her recent mariage; yet it had not been for want of trying. After considerable thought, she decided that the same problems had been encountered in all her relationships.

At this point, the pain of her recent divorce overcame her and she spent a few tearful minutes of sheer desperation. This was followed by a feeling of revulsion at the whole idea of analyzing her past. Divorces were common enough, after all. There was no point in raking over the past; she was better off on her own anyway. But her mind refused to leave her in peace. She remembered the injunction to act rather than to think and the need to put time into the problem. Finally, she decided to spend half an hour each day thinking about one of the sub-headings in the list, starting with stability and ending with mutual help.

In practice, the work did not prove easy; several times she almost gave up, overwhelmed by feelings of helplessness. But there was satisfaction too, when aspects of her relationships that she had previously refused to face came within the grasp of her mind. The past had gone, but at least it could be faced up to and, perhaps, understood. Occasionally, amidst the pain and confusion of her search, there was a flash of excited understanding when a recurring pattern of behavior or habit of thought was recognized. But, on the whole, it was a traumatic experience.

When it was over, she had come to a conclusion that was, to her, surprising. Of all the headings in the list, two of them—

stability and resources—caused the most reaction in her. She determined to devote her half-hour sessions to these two subjects alone.

Stability gave her a lot of trouble. She felt the need for things to be safe and predictable and stable, certainly, but who did not? The deeper implications eluded her for some time until she realized that, in her mind, stability and resources went together. She felt she needed possessions and money to guarantee her stability and that without them there was a danger that her universe would somehow break up. She seemed to need the weight of possessions to keep her psychological wholeness; without them she felt she was nothing. Considering the matter brought back memories of her marriage and previous relationships, the fears and the worries. Not a pleasant experience, but it did bring a degree of insight she had never before achieved.

She realized her constant concern about the safety of her husband's job and promotion prospects, her over-careful budgeting, her rejection of new experiences, her clinging possessiveness and the claustrophobic way they lived had finally made even her easygoing husband feel trapped. This was a revelation to her. She had aimed her attention at a relationship problem; but this had led her to quite another area.

Belinda still had problems. In fact sometimes she seemed to have more problems; but a degree of understanding had been added. She was moving and the process would not stop there. And, like John, she was alive again.

· · ·

The occult or magical component in these quite ordinary actions is the *willed intention*. Willed intention followed by action within a strict discipline of time is the formula. Should you decide to undertake a similar task in your own life, remember to keep your sense of humor. Be kind to yourself. You are a very important person with a unique destiny yet to fulfill.

Destiny

Destiny makes available skills and aptitudes that expand you and increase your self-expression. Karma restricts you, makes you what you are *not*, and tries to keep you like that. People's destinies are quite individual but fall into well-defined categories. In this respect, destinies are rather like faces. Each human face is unique, yet it can be classified in a general way as round, oval, triangular, and so on. Individual destiny is divisible into types of aptitude and ability.

For example, you may be a natural scientist. This does not mean that you are born each life with a knowledge of chemistry or physics. But it does imply that you have a natural aptitude for logical thought, classification, observation and deduction. An artist type would have the ability to represent natural forces, human emotions, and aspiration in some medium or other—paint, clay, music, drama and so on. Early errors can so distort and corrupt the original spiritual drive that you believe yourself to be what you are not and act accordingly. An artist type can try to force himself or herself into the mode of a scientist, or the scientist can attempt to work through the mask of an administrator. In such cases, destiny is always trying to find a channel and sometimes the results can be bizarre. If you work within your destiny profile you are a potential genius. Karma breeds frustration, and, at best, mediocrity.

"Peter" is a bass player in a band. Competent, loyal and reliable he certainly is, but equally certainly he is not a top-grade musician. However, he arranges the band's schedules and other business brilliantly. From being an unknown and near bankrupt outfit when he joined, his efforts have made the band secure, well equipped and financially sound. Everyone recognizes that he has a genius for organization. This is true, for he is a natural administrator. Unfortunately, his karma has made him a merely mediocre musician.

"John" is in electronics, working on the synthesis of musical sound. But he plays a synthesizer far better than he can design one. Here is a karmic scientist, but a destiny artist.

Now this book is concerned with the practical aspects of the Qabalah. It is written for those who want to *do* something rather than just talk about it. So it is understandable if some readers wonder why so much stress has been laid upon karma and its attendant woes and problems. But occultism deals with the whole of a person, not just the mind. If you hope to use the Qabalah to expand your horizons and explore your inner worlds, you should realize that, initially at least, you will be experiencing yourself. Karma has made you what you are. Destiny represents what you should be. Karma belongs to the past—destiny to the future. When you start to work with the Qabalistic system and are serious about it, changes will occur within the "windswept spaces of the soul." The changes will be within the very substance of yourself.

Over the door of the Temple of the Mysteries is inscribed the words, "Know Thyself." A study of karma and destiny is vital to this goal of self-knowledge, which gives admission to the temple.

CHAPTER ELEVEN

The Anatomy of Ritual

A RITUAL IS a living symbol. Like all symbols, a ceremonial working is a form which represents one or more realities, but—unlike the sort of symbols we have been dealing with up to now—a ritual involves our physical and etheric levels as well as the emotional and mental planes. It is an extension from the inner "outward" into matter.

The point of all occult operations should be *change on the physical plane*. But there is no need to limit change only to the result of formal esoteric workings. A change of attitude, for example, should result in a change in the way of life on the physical plane. An idea—a mental form—becomes a physical reality, a new invention perhaps. Naturally, a system of working that is able to clothe an abstract concept or a subtle force with a vehicle on mental, emotional, etheric and physical levels at the same time is already well on the way to a complete expression of change in earth, and a properly executed ritual can do just this. This is the secret of success in properly executed occult ritual: a Jacob's ladder leads from heaven to earth and we can use it to by-pass the twists and torts of our deviations to express a perfection in microcosm.

It has been said that if geometrical symbols are the letters in the alphabet of the mysteries, then compound symbols are

words—personalized symbols can form sentences and dynamic
symbols can make whole chapters in the great *Book of Life*. The
dramatic ceremonial symbol is actually all these things and more,
and shows forth—in miniature—the "Great Work."

Types of Ritual Working

There are three basic ways in which we can use our several bodies
as a unified whole to build our own Jacob's ladder.

Qabalistic

As the name suggests, this method is based on the monotheistic
approach of the Qabalah. An appropriate sephirotic temple is
jointly formulated in the imagination by the participants, usually
helped by some degree of appropriate physical-plane symbolism.
Generally, there is a minimum of physical movement; but much
use is made of the Hebrew God-names and other appropriate
"words of power." The words of the ceremony guide the visual
imagination and mood of those present, thus making an inner-
plane form. The officers in the rite meditate strongly upon some
desired sephirotic force (or quality) and "inject" it into the prepared form by sounding-forth the Hebrew name appropriate to
the god-form, archangel, or angel chosen to focus the force of
the sephirah. In capable hands, this can produce extraordinary
results. However, it does call for experience and a high degree of
ability, and is not a method for the novice.

Egyptian

This form of working is outwardly polytheistic, using as it does
the many god-forms of the ancient Egyptian mysteries; properly
understood, however, it is monotheistic, the inner priesthood
believing in the idea of "One God with many faces." A certain
amount of group visualization is employed to set the scene, but

greatest use is made of the god-forms and of certain formal gestures, symbolically characteristic of the God whose force is being invoked. The appropriate god-forms are built up as if positioned in certain parts of the temple and, at the climax of the working, one or more of the ritual officers "assumes" the god-form. This ritual consists in mentally coalescing the visualized form of the god with the officer's physical form, imagining its body to surround and inter-penetrate the officer's body. Most important is that the god's head fuse with the officer of the rite. If this tricky procedure is successfully accomplished, then the priest or priestess becomes imbued with the force of the god and his or her mouth "speaks with the voice of Horus" or whoever. Again, not a method for the aspiring magician!

Greek

The third approach uses music, verse and movement, first to represent, and then to invoke the desired force. Stylized ritual movement, often in the form of a dance, depicts the force. Evocative poetry and chanting stir the imagination, and the power of the god is given expression in the mime and movement of the choreography. Some examples of this method are highly stylized and organized, but it also lends itself to informal and spontaneous expression.

The three basic methods correspond to levels of consciousness: the Qabalistic corresponds to the abstract mind, the Egyptian corresponds to the concrete mind, and the Greek corresponds to the emotions. Naturally, even the Greek has its abstract aspect in the one life from which all things come; and all three have the physical/etheric levels present in the bodies of those taking part. And no method will work at all unless the feelings are roused, for emotion is "the ass that carries the Ark." What is really meant by saying that a particular approach corresponds to a certain aspect of the psyche is that a certain level of the mind is used to motivate and control the operation; but *all* the levels are active, otherwise there could be no Jacob's ladder.

Subjective and Objective Aspects of Ritual

Every facet of human life has a subjective (personal or inner) aspect and an objective (or outer) side. Ritual is no exception. Any participant in a ceremony will react to what is going on. We will experience feelings, think thoughts, get impressions, and so on. Others present will also have feelings, thoughts and impressions, but these need not be (and probably will not be) the same for any two people. On the other hand, some of our ideas and feelings may be shared by all those present, which suggests reactions to something that exists in its own right "outside" the personal universe of the participants. In the same way, a witness to a street accident will have personal reactions to the event, pity perhaps, or reactions to the sight of blood. A doctor tending the wounded would probably have quite different subjective reactions, and a policeman would have very different ones again. Yet all would probably agree on certain points, the fact that there had been an accident, the presence of a car, a driver, an injured pedestrian, the presence of blood, etc. These are objective elements, what the policeman might call "the facts."

The question of objectivity is an important matter in practical occultism and one that causes a lot of trouble among beginners. It is not uncommon to hear the label "true" applied to objective phenomena and "imaginary" to any inner experience. This is neither helpful nor accurate as it tends to de-value personal experience. If by subjective we mean "within the self," and by objective, "shared by others," then quite simply, subjective means personal, and objective means collective. Both have validity. A ritual worked by one person, or even two, might be rich in subjective experience and have little objective content; yet it could be highly effective.

Some rituals are designed to induce subjective reactions to the almost total exclusion of the objective. An example of this type of working would be in group development or regeneration where a particular force would be induced into the ceremony, the participants reacting according to their capacity and past experience. Another working might stress the objective side, being constructed to provide a common experience to all those present.

However, no one is an island. The subjective overflows into the objective and the personal soul into the group soul. Some philosophers would even argue that objectivity is simply a postulate or common agreement on what is to be considered as fact. Be that as it may, the budding ritualist should clearly understand that all working is—at least initially—entirely subjective. Magic works upon the soul, not upon matter directly. But, when a chord within the soul induces a response from the soul of nature, then the subjective has become objectified, and the personal life receives an influx of force and ideas from the greater life. Such moments are rarely forgotten.

Symbolism and Ritual

Symbols of one sort or another have been mentioned in almost all the chapters of this book. However, no matter how strong your urge to get down to business and practice what you have learned, theory must always be kept in mind. Superstition has been defined as performing an observance without knowing why; in practical occultism this is inexcusable and possibly dangerous.

If we get some order into our thinking by using the four worlds of the Qabalist as a guide, then we must regard Yetzirah as the "home" of most of the symbols and glyphs we have been talking about. Yetzirah is the world of feelings and emotions, an older phase than this one, a state that ruled before the discipline of speech produced that specialization of consciousness we call the concrete mind. Symbols are nearer to the inner core than speech. This world of Yetzirah is like Atziluth in some ways, but on a lower level. Both Yetzirah and Atziluth are dynamic and free-moving; Atziluth in terms of force and Yetzirah in terms of form. An archetypal symbol, whose natural level is Yetzirah, is simply a construction which mirrors some fundamental activity of the Atziluthic world. If you understand this principle, it may give an insight into the way sympathetic magic works. Considering the symbols we have encountered so far, you will see that they divide into four fairly well-defined categories and these categories correspond with the type of force or being represented. The dramatic or ceremonial type of symbol is the most complex because it is an extension into the world of Assiah (the physical universe) of the dynamic symbols of Yetzirah. See Table 6.

Table 6. Symbolic Correspondences

Type or Symbol	Classification	Example	Qabalistic World
Geometrical	Abstract force	Point, Line, Circle	Atziluth
Compound	Organized force	Anhk, Cross	Briah
Personalized	Intelligent force	Archangel, Isis-Osiris	
Dynamic	Symbol-chain	Pathworkings, Magical Images	Yetzirah
Dramatic	Force-pattern	Ceremonial, Ritual, Invocation/Evocation, Initiation	Assiah

By now it should be clear that the ultimate object of all legitimate occult work is to *realize* the true plan—for yourself, for your group, for humanity and for this planet as a whole. To realize means "to make real." And real means "actually existing, objective, not merely apparent, occurring in fact" (Oxford Dictionary). Dramatic symbolism, usually called "ritual" or "ceremonial," makes the final and vital link from the inner worlds to the physical plane. In ritual, the symbolic pattern which is used to channel inner forces is not "merely apparent" (a mental picture) but "actually existing," "occurring in fact," real and living.

A ritual can be (and often is) performed by one person. Two or three people make a perfectly adequate ritual team for many purposes, while other cases may demand half a dozen or more participants. In all cases, however, the one or several taking part are—for the period of the ritual—exemplifying a symbol or a symbol-chain. The idea or force represented is being grounded.

You now know that you will apply the teachings to your daily life and continually attempt to give expression to your ideals and realizations. Performing a ritual designed to express the ideal of truth in no way removes the need to exemplify that ideal in life. If the ritual symbol constructed to represent truth was a good one, and if the ceremony was properly performed, then, for the duration of the ritual, a perfect form for "truth" existed in Malkuth. Excellent! But that fact does not remove the need to ground that ideal in the life and environment.

The temple is rather like the laboratory of the industrial chemist. Here, the product is prepared under ideal conditions; but before it can be put on the market as a household commodity, it must first be taken out of the laboratory; otherwise, it remains unknown and unusable. Ritual is a very potent tool. It can be used whenever there is a need to express an ideal or to contact, focus, and direct power. Its applications include personal and group development, individual regeneration and healing, as well as the healing of the nations.

Rituals in Practice

Ritual "furniture" is made up of the physical symbols used in your ceremonies. In order to practice a ritual, you should use the particular ritual objects that pertain to the system you have chosen to work with. Do not mix systems; i.e., do not use Qabalistic god-names with Egyptian imagery, etc. Your rituals are best carried out in places set aside for the purpose, though this is not always possible. Experience shows that when ceremonies are regularly performed in one place, the atmosphere becomes "tuned-up." After repeated use, the symbols become surrounded by an etheric field, a sort of subtle counterpart of the physical symbol. From an inner plane viewpoint, the entire temple becomes a pattern of forces joining the furniture into a geometrical form. When performing a ceremony in such surroundings, much of the hard work of preparing the atmosphere is unnecessary because forms build easily in sheltered conditions and take on a solidity not easy to obtain when you have no real center.

Obviously, these are conditions that few solitary workers can enjoy these days. However, much can be achieved by improvisation, *clear intention* and profundity of feeling. The conditions described here are realistic for an established ritual group but are ideals for the solitary student. They will serve as a yardstick.

Any place used to perform ritual becomes, for the duration of the rite at least, a temple, even if it is a converted bedroom. The remarks which follow, although applying to permanent temples, can be applied in many cases to temporary accommodation for ceremonies.

Ideally, the room should be large enough to accommodate necessary equipment and the officers who are to perform the rite. A square shape is good. Traditionally, the temple is orientated to a compass point—north, east, south, and west. That is, each quarter of the room is assigned to its appropriate compass point. One wall becomes the eastern quarter, its opposite, the west, and the other two walls become the north and the south. It is not strictly necessary for the orientation to be to the compass points:

if one quarter of the room is considered as the east then, from the inner-world point of view it *is* the east and the other quarters take up their appropriate significance. Nevertheless, if it is at all possible, it is best to align to the physical compass point as certain rituals involving etheric and elemental forces do require actual east-west force flows.

In the system operated by many groups, the eastern quarter is alloted to the element air, the west to water, the south to fire and the north to earth. Other systems sometimes vary this assignment. The four quarters follow the clockwise movement of the sun and the sequence of the four seasons of the year. The sun rises in the east, is highest in the south, sets in the west and is invisible in the north. Likewise, to the east is assigned spring and all new growth; to the south, maturity; to the west, decline and death; and to the north, the inner world state between lives. Thus this aspect of temple symbolism is a pageant of the progress of the sun of God and the soul of mankind.

The roof of the temple for most people these days is not some vaulted dome but the ceiling of the room they use for this purpose. It symbolizes all supernal things, all things which are "higher" or more "inner" than the level of the current working. For example, if a rite of Yesod were being worked, the ceiling would represent the higher sephiroth from which, presumably, the inner inspiration for the rite was drawn.

The floor is often taken to depict the level below which the focus of the ceremony is aimed. In the example of a Yesod ritual, the floor would represent Malkuth. In fact it is a good idea to make the floor mean the physical universe in all cases. One of the commonest faults of ritual working lies in a failure to realize the forces invoked in earth.

A temple may be used to perform a wide variety of workings so it is restrictive to use color in a definite way. In practice, the floor is best carpeted in a one-tone darkish shade, black, brown or somber green; it should not intrude upon the eye. The ceiling should not focus attention either and is often painted a dark blue or indigo. In this way in a dimly lit room it gives the impression of receding upwards. The walls are best treated with a neutral color. A certain amount of reflected light is useful; too much can be disturbing. A mid-gray is sometimes used and avoids the color bias problem.

Everyone present at a ritual must have somewhere to sit, and it is common practice for the actual ceremonial officers to have special chairs to mark their appointment in the rite. These chairs are often known as "thrones" and are of a different pattern to those used to seat the other members. Many rituals demand an officer in each of the four quarters, and each throne is placed exactly in the center of one of the walls. A throne has a great deal of significance in ceremonies and represents the "office" even when the physical officer is not occupying it. When outside the temple, an officer is a person and speaks as a person, but when he or she occupies such a seat the officer speaks "ex cathedra" (from the throne) with the power and authority of the office. A great number of workings are controlled from the east and the throne of the principal officer resides there. This seat has exceptional significance. It is the seat of the hierophant and, in initiatory rites, often depicts the power behind the veil, the inner-plane order from which the physical plane group receives its contacts and its mandate to initiate.

The central symbol in any temple is the altar. In orthodox Christianity it is placed in the east; in temples of the mysteries it is usually situated in the center. Thus it can be visualized as the focus of the forces of the four quarters, or the central boss of the four-spoked wheel of force. All altars are places of sacrifice. In olden times they sacrificed by blood and burnt offerings; now the offering is on subtler levels, but equally real, as the neophyte rapidly finds out. At first you offer up your deviations for transmutation into the gold of the spirit; later you offer up yourself for the purposes of the great work. Physically, the altar in the Western tradition is in the proportions of a double cube "as high as the navel of a six foot man." To allay speculation about the physical attributes of initiates, it can be said that in practice the altar is three feet high and eighteen inches square! Often it is made in the form of a cupboard so that the special symbols of a ritual can be stored away there when the ceremony is over. The altar may be covered by a cloth whose color or form has significance in the ceremony. On the altar top may be a ritual lamp and certain other symbols.

In the sections on the Qabalah, reference has been made to a division of the Tree into three vertical pillars, the two outer ones representing the universal principles of polarity and the center one representing consciousness. In lodges of the Western Mysteries, the pillar symbolism is often used. In complementary colors, one black/one white, or one green/one gold, they represent psychological as well as cosmic principles. Their position in the temple varies according to the needs of the working. Generally they are between six and seven feet high, of tubular construction on a heavy square base.

Ceremonies are normally carried out by artificial light because this can be controlled in a way that daylight cannot. And the delicate etheric forms built up in the working, especially around the principal symbols, can easily be dispersed by excess light. In fact, one of the easiest ways to break up debased or otherwise unwanted etheric matter is to expose it to very bright light, preferably from the sun, othewise from an ultraviolet lamp. Nevertheless, despite the need for restraint, some light is necessary for most workings. You need to be able to see to move about and, perhaps, to read. Candles are generally used to light the temple because they give a soft and gentle light and because they provide a naked flame. Flame is symbolically important for a variety of reasons but has another contribution to make as well. The conversion of gases into light and heat seems to liberate a measure of etheric substance which helps to provide raw material for forms on this level of being.

Like everything else in the temple, the number of lights is significant. For example, in a ritual concerning the four elements, there might well be four officers each devoted to bringing through the force of one element. Each officer could be provided with a candle alongside his throne. A fifth light, probably on the altar, could be used to symbolize spirit—the one life from which the elements derive their existence. Sometimes colored glass covers are used for the candles and the colors are significant. Certain types of rite may be performed by the dim light of one tiny point of flame floating upon consecrated oil in a hanging lamp. The thing to remember is that lights have a precise function in a ceremony and are not to be regarded as ornamental or merely functional.

Much Western occultism is fourfold in its basic symbolism. Reference has already been made to the four elements and the four quarters of the temple. It is also important to realize that the four principles apply not only to elemental life on its natural level, but to all the spheres of manifestation. The best way of considering them is by analogy with the four Qabalistic worlds which can represent four conditions of life on any level. Likewise, the four elements in Malkuth are the pale reflections of the four holy living creatures in Kether. The fourfold elemental symbolism so common in Western ritual practice must be considered as something altogether more all-embracing than at first appears to be the case.

It is fairly common to see the symbols of the four elements hanging from the appropriate walls of the temple. In the east is an upward-pointing triangle with a horizontal bar across it, representing air. In the south is a plain up-pointing triangle depicting fire. The western wall bears a down-pointing triangle symbolizing water, while in the north is a barred down-pointing triangle representing earth. Sometimes they are colored in the appropriate yellow, red, blue and black.

Each element also has its own special symbolic object and these are sometimes placed upon the altar. Traditions vary in their particular attributions, but air is commonly represented by a knife, water by a cup, fire by a wand, and earth by a disc. Several arrangements are possible.

This completes the brief outline of basic ritual furniture. Many additions to the list could be made but are so totally dependent upon the level and type of the ceremony being performed, that it is pointless to include them.

Finally, one thing should be kept in mind—simplicity. Use few symbols rather than many.

Robes

Robes are not classed as "furniture," in a ritual but they are sufficiently important to deserve some attention. The principal officers and other participants in ceremonial working often wear robes. The object is threefold; first, a robe by its color and symbolism can depict the force of the officer who wears it. Second, ritual robing produces a sort of anonymity—the personality may be rich or poor, doctor or dustman—but it disappears behind the robes and there is revealed someone who can do anything or be anyone. It is as if the mask of the everyday is replaced by another mask, an altogether wider expression of the Self, which allows the being to expand and live more intensely than does the uniform of everyday use. Third, a robe is often used to indicate an office (such as Hierophant), a grade, or status within the structure of the group. In a properly constituted group, grade is not used as a proclamation of imagined worth or as a means of impressing others, but as an outward sign of the continuity of the mystery structure and an incentive to press onward. Robes can be home-made and may range from the simplest shift to very elaborate constructions of velvet and silk richly embroidered with symbolic devices.

Head-dresses of various types are sometimes worn with robes. There are many different patterns from a simple copper fillet about the hair to a nemyss (or nemes) in the style of the pharoahs of old. A belt or girdle is sometimes worn about the waist, often made of thin rope or silk cord. Sometimes colored, the girdle is always symbolic and its meaning varies enormously with the system being worked.

Last of the robing accoutrements are the sandals. The temple is consecrated; therefore its floor is holy ground, not to be trodden on by boots or shoes. The sandals, which may have a symbolic color, are often quite ordinary pliable, soft-soled bedroom slippers. For some workings, sandals are dispensed with and bare feet are the order of the day.

Robing requirements vary with the system and type of working, but no matter how simple or elaborate the vestments, they must be bought or made for ritual purposes only and never used in any other way, or displayed to those outside the ritual group for which they were intended to be used. There are sound psychological and magical reasons for this precaution.

Incense

Incense is of great value to ritual. To paraphase the poet, scents have a far more profound effect than either sights or sounds. Traditionally, there is a whole alphabet of correspondences between the many forces and factors of manifestation and the aromatic gums and sweet oils employed in ritual. In Qabalistic terms, there is a scent assigned to each sephirah and path upon the Tree. Many of the attributes are sound, but some are dubious and appear to have been selected for the most slender of reasons. The subject is a complicated one and the many occultists who worship correspondences and tables of symbols more than the realities they are supposed to represent do little to simplify the matter.

Beginners would do well to ignore the contention and select from the recommended gums and oils one that to them really epitomizes the force or factor with which they wish to work. If a scent has been selected for work on Netzach, it should always be used for that sphere and for no other. In this way the full evocative power of perfume can be used to the full. When the scent is detected, the mind will select all the feelings, experiences, and emotions that have accumulated from past contact with the sphere. The mood will definitely be tuned to the work in hand.

There is another use to which incense is sometimes put. The smoke of burning gums or oils is occasionally used to provide material for the manifestation of a force which already has a mental form provided for it and etheric matter to clothe that form. The scented smoke is employed to provide an easily moulded physical shell which can be temporarily utilized for the purposes of the rite. Such work is rarely necessary.

The Human Element

Among all this ritual paraphernalia move human beings, the greatest ceremonial instruments of all. The main purpose of ritual furniture and other aids is to assist concentration, to provide foci for joint concentration in the case of a group working. Individual work does not call for their use to the same degree, and an experienced ritualist can dispense with most of them. However, to anyone gaining experience of this type of work, a careful selection and intelligent use of ritual symbols can be of great value.

Ritual paraphernalia is of little use if the human element is inadequate. It is the task of the ritual officers to contact, channel, and direct the chosen inner-plane forces. To do this satisfactorily, a chain of symbols must be set up and used in the manner described earlier. Students can be trained in ceremonial work only up to a certain degree and not beyond it. They can be taught to build and maintain the required forms, for that is all ritual itself really is—the construction and maintenance of forms. But the best car designer in the world can do no more than admire the static perfection of his creation unless there exists a fuel to drive the car. Life is the fuel of ritual. Without the ability to contact life-force at the required level, ritualists are in the same position. In fact they are worse off, for without the in-spiring force, their forms will waver and vanish like the mists of the morning.

Now this ability to contact life in its essence is dependent upon two things; evolutionary experience and training, and freedom from psychological blockages. With goodwill, honesty and a willingness to face yourself, the second obstacle can be surmounted, at least to a degree. But the primary requirement—inner development—is an index of the state of your Higher Self, the vehicle of past evolution. Occult training can help you unfold to the present limit of your capacities; it can indicate the way ahead and help you tread it, but it cannot make silk purses out of sows' ears, no matter how enthusiastic the sow or how gorgeous her raiment.

However, assuming even a modest ability to contact the One Life in some department, and the possession of a healthy un-superstitious attitude to symbols, much can be done. The most important consideration is a clear understanding of the human role. You are the most marvellous ritual object. You are a whole temple full of furniture and symbols, all connected up to a transformer station which is linked to life itself. Training in ceremonial method is the craft which teaches the use of this wonderful tool.

Clear thinking and strong, free emotions are obviously essential to the successful ceremonialist, but so is the state of your body and the way you handle it. For example, your body should be healthy, strong, and trained not to react unduly when you make reasonable demands upon it. When at rest, seated in a chair, your back should be straight, your head properly poised upon your neck, your hands at rest and your body relaxed yet alert. This is simple for some, but surprisingly difficult for many others. Movement should be *purposeful*, smooth and unhurried. Speech should be clear, well modulated and embody reality. Above all, while showing forth by your speech and movement vast forces and ancient truths, you should remain completely in present time. You must never lose sight of what you are, where you are, and what you are doing, *now*.

CHAPTER TWELVE

Basic Ritual Exercises

THE OBJECT OF the practical work which follows is to introduce you the co-ordination of your several levels. A great deal can certainly be gained from the proper application of the exercises we will discuss, but the only way to become a really competent ritualist is to work ritual and, ultimately to receive training and experience from a functioning ritual group. What these exercises *will* do is to teach you the fundamentals from which a ceremony is constructed. As such, their practice is invaluable.

To enable you to do justice to yourself as well as to the work, the following conditions should be met: clothing should be loose and comfortable, feet shod in soft slippers of some sort, and the room temperature adequate. There should be a clear floor space of six feet square or more, you should shut out the daylight, and you need complete privacy for the fifteen minutes or so required for the work. Noise level should be as low as possible but earplugs can be used for some of the practices.

Exercise 1

For this exercise you need an upright chair—preferably hard—and earplugs if you want them. Normal daylight or artificial light is allowed.

First you must practice a simple form of breathing rhythm called the fourfold breath. This is not a yoga exercise, just a simple way of getting comfortable, relaxed and calm. Simply breathe in gently to the slow count of four, then relax, letting the air remain in the lungs to the count of two. Next, gently breathe out to the count of four; finally relax with lungs empty for two counts. Breathe in again to the four count as before and continue. Find your own best rhythm and never ever strain. If you experience discomfort at any point in the breathing cycle, then you have got something wrong; probably your count is too extended. Try reducing the duration. Practice this exercise until you are comfortable and the breathing is automatic.

Now position your chair with its back to the source of light if possible. Stand with your back to the chair in a poised yet relaxed manner. Imagine that you hear a voice coming from in front of you telling you to sit. Then with one smooth movement, putting all your attention on what you are doing, place yourself in the chair. Put your hands palm down along the top of your thighs. Look straight in front of you and breathe steadily to the fourfold rhythm as described above. Be absolutely still and attempt at the same time to attain an inner quiet. Repeat this exercise until you think you can do it well, and would not mind demonstrating it to another person.

Exercise 2

First position your chair with its back to the source of the light. Stand with your back to the chair but about six paces in front of it. Practice walking backward on hearing the imaginary order and sit in the chair as before. When walking backwards, it is important to keep the head high, the pace measured and to avoid the temptation to look behind you. Again try to achieve a smooth and continuous movement. Then become quite still and breath steadily in the fourfold rhythm.

Exercise 3

The final version of this basic exercise requires the services of a broom handle, with or without its head. Stand, as in exercise two, six paces in front of the chair. Hold the broomstick in front of you in both hands, exactly as if it were a sword, point upwards. Pace backwards to the chair holding the "sword" absolutely vertical, pause for a brief moment, get a mental picture of someone alongside you similarly armed. When the imaginary person sits, you do likewise, in synchronism. When you are seated, let the image fade and continue to hold the weapon point up and quite still. The hilt should be grasped at the bottom by one hand resting in the lap. The other hand can steady the "sword" at a point higher up the hilt. Become still and breathe as before. Try to remain in this state for several minutes. A clock or kitchen timer is useful here.

Exercise 4

For this exercise, mark a circle on the floor with chalk (it brushes out of carpets). This circle should be as large in diameter as possible. Stand on the line facing the source of light with your hands clasped before you in the attitude of prayer. Imagine a voice telling you to walk. When you hear it, turn and walk clockwise around the circle with regular steps, breathing in time to your step. Walk four times round the circle clockwise, then stop and face inwards.

• • •

A variation on this exercise is to clasp your hands across your chest in the manner that the dead are laid out and proceed as before. The knack is in the regular pacing and synchronized breath. Difficulties in balance may be experienced at first.

• • •

Another useful practice based upon the same circumambulation is to choose a sentence from a book or newspaper at random and recite it in time with the step. The sentence should be short enough to repeat several times in a four-circuit exercise. The words should be spoken in a low but clear voice with a rhythmical delivery. Hands should be crossed upon your chest as before.

• • •

The final variation on the circling practice is to half-fill a wine glass with water and hold it in front of you on a level with your eyes, using both hands with a thumb and forefinger of each hand on either side of the bowl of the glass. The other fingers should be together and facing forwards. Circle four times clockwise as before, keeping your eyes fixed upon the glass. On completion of the final circle, face inward and raise the glass as high as you comfortably can, hold it still for a moment and then lower it.

Exercise 5

Your hands are the finest magical implements. They can be used to heal and to bless, to consecrate, or to direct a flow of force. Unless your daily work gives your hands ample exercise, you would do well to find exercises to keep them supple and to develop their muscular system. This exercise uses two hand positions, cupped and flat. It requires a wineglass half full of water and a candle. If there is daylight, it should be excluded as far as possible.

Draw your circle as before. Light the candle and place it in view but outside the circle. It doesn't matter where you put the candle, as long as it is outside the circle. You are only using it as soft light, not as a ritual object. Place the half-full wineglass of water upon a stool or chair in the center of the circle. Stand facing the chair inside the circle and also facing the light. Raise your left arm pointing upwards in line with your body. Bend back your hand from the wrist and try to form a shallow cup with your fingers which should be together. Lower your right hand, palm down, fingers together over the glass. Your feet should be slightly apart to preserve balance. Breathe steadily and fairly deeply in the fourfold rhythm. Now imagine that the life-force (or whatever other name you care to give it) is condensing in the air over the cupped fingers of your left hand in a golden haze. See it gathering as a vital, sparkling liquid in the cup of your hand. Let it pour down within your left arm, across the top of your chest and down your right arm to the palm of your hand. From the palm it pours out in a vibrant golden stream into the liquid in the glass. The liquid seems to boil under the impact of this energy. After a short time, let the activity slowly die away. Lower your hands to your side. Pause for a moment; then raise the glass in the manner described in the last exercise. See the water in the glass as full of radiant particles of energy. Lower the glass and replace it on the chair. Pause for a short time, then leave the circle and extinguish the candle.

• • •

This exercise uses the powers of the visual imagination in co-ordination with the ritual gestures. An exercise such as this will demand considerable practice before ease and confident operation are achieved. Practical ceremonial is made up of many such actions, therefore this type of drill will repay attention.

Exercise 6

This exercise uses your hand as a pointing, focussing, and directing instrument. Set up one chair with its front feet on one side of a circle and on it place the lighted candle. Put another chair

similarly on the opposite side of the circle and on it rest any small
object, such as an ornament. Exclude any daylight as far as
possible and take your place within the circle in the center, with
your back to the light. Stand with your arms at your side for a
moment, breathing in the fourfold manner. As you are doing
this, imagine the light from the candle entering your back and
accumulating under increasing pressure in the area of your right
shoulder. Now slowly raise your right arm and point it, absolutely
straight, at the object on the far chair. The first two fingers should
be extended, together, as pointers. The other fingers must be
folded into your palm and retained by your thumb. Now imagine
the pent-up energy in your shoulder as being suddenly released,
flowing with great force down your outstretched right arm to your
directing fingers where it is released in an intense beam toward
the object. Try this several times, relaxing in between with the
breathing practice.

Communication Exercise

Effective living is largely a matter of effective communication.
Occultism is condensed life and ritual should exemplify perfected
form. Ritual, properly executed, is also a demonstration of perfected communication. For this exercise select a poem or short
piece of prose, preferably of a stirring or evocative nature, and
read through it enough times to become thoroughly familiar with
it. There is no need to learn it by heart. Two chairs should be
set up on the edges of the circle, facing each other. In the center
of the circle, on the floor, place a lighted candle. A second candle
is arranged to the left of one of the chairs in such a position that
it will give enough light to see to read. Sit in this chair and
breathe in the fourfold manner for a few minutes. While doing
this, build up the image of a member of the opposite sex as if he
or she were sitting in the opposite chair. When you have done
this as well as you are able, start reading the script. Scan a

sentence or line at a time, then raise your eyes and deliver it to the simulacrum opposite you. Try to pitch your voice slightly lower than usual. *Feel* what you are saying and let your feelings travel, carried by your words, to their destination. See if you can imagine some sort of a return flow. Ideally, of course, this practice should be carried out by two people, each taking a turn at the delivery, but this can rarely be achieved. The main purpose of this exercise is to accustom yourself to the use of speech as a vehicle for feeling. It also helps you become familiar with the techniques of polarity in ritual. Success depends upon natural ability and plenty of relaxed practice.

The Pillars Exercise

This exercise involves both physical movement and use of the visual imagination. It concerns the pillars. In this exercise, the chairs act as foci for the images which are constructed by your mind.

For this, you will need four chairs (or 3 and a small table) and one candle. Choose one quarter of the room and call it the east. Place a chair or small table there to support the candle. Put another chair in the west; this is your seat. A three-foot diameter circle is created so its center is on a line between the two chairs, at the half-way mark. Position the other two chairs at right-angles to the east-west line with their back legs touching the circle so that they face each other back-to-back across the circle. Let these two chairs represent the two pillars.

Light the candle and sit down. Fourfold breathe for half a dozen cycles and when you feel that you are calm and stable, let the two chairs become the bases of two great pillars in your mind. The one on your right is white, and the left one is black. See them towering upwards; imagine the incredible tension that must exist between these vast representations of universal and personal polarity. Think of all the complementaries which these principles represent. See, in contrast to their size and height, the narrow space between them. Sense their power, and as you do so, slowly rise. Taking short measured and rhythmic steps, enter the circle and pass between them. Do not pause, but attempt to feel the tension between them like a tangible thing through which you move. Stand for a moment before the light in the east, then extinguish the candle.

Sound and Silence

Place a candle at the center of a six-foot circle and set a chair on the edge of the circle. Now stand before the chair and sit in the manner described in exercise 1. Breathe as before. Become as still as you are able. Now listen to the silence. Ignore any distracting background noises and concentrate in a relaxed manner on the quality which is silence. Refuse to recognize anything which is not of this essence. Do not continue this exercise for too long; just give yourself a time to get the feel of silence. Listening is a vital part of the communication process.

Speaking Exercise

For this a tape recorder is useful, but not essential. Sit in a chair with the candle positioned to give light for reading. Take a poem or a good piece of prose. The Old Testament is good, but the Highway Code would almost do as well. Breathe in the fourfold manner for a while, then read. Try for a good measured delivery, as well-modulated and rhythmic as the text allows. Try not to let your voice drop at the end of a phrase or sentence. Control your breathing. Now, if you have a recorder, play it back. If you haven't heard yourself before, you may get a shock—perhaps pleasant. Note your faults and repeat the exercise trying to correct them. Do not forget to remain still while reading.

The Altar

You need a piece of furniture about three feet high with a flat top. A chest of drawers would do quite well. Clear the top and place the candle on it about a foot back from the edge. Position a chair about four feet from it. Light the candle and sit down. Breathe for a few cycles and imagine the piece of furniture to be an altar carrying a sacred lamp. Perceive it as the center of all things in the universe and in the soul of humanity. Mentally approach it as to a great heart, a vast mind, as a focus of power, or, preferably, all these things at one time. Now walk slowly towards it in this attitude of mind and stand before the light. Place your hands upon the altar surface side by side and palms down. Bow your head and be aware. After a short time, put out the light.

The Qabalistic Cross

This ritual gesture is so well publicized that it is in danger of being under-rated. While all the foregoing exercises have been devised for training purposes, this one is actually used in ceremonial work. In it an equal-armed cross is traced both physically and in the imagination upon the front of the body. Esoterically, it affirms the rule of God or the spirit in all human bodies and in the universe.

Draw the six-foot circle and place a chair at the edge. Light a candle and position it on another chair at the far side of the circle. Sit, breathe, and establish poise. Try to realize yourself as an entity whose physical form is but the terminal of a being whose essential essence is eternally rooted in a world of infinite power, absolute harmony and eternal duration. Feel yourself as a being capable of wielding spiritual power in the world of matter. Then, when you are ready, rise and stand with arms at your sides. Keep your left arm by your side with its fingers together. Now raise your right arm with the first two fingers outstretched together and the other fingers folded in and retained by the thumb. Touch your forehead, saying "Unto Thee—." Now move your hand down the center line of your body and touch your solar plexus, saying, "Is the Kingdom—." Now touch your right shoulder and say, "And the Power—," then your left shoulder saying, "And the Glory—." Finally clasp your hands together with fingers intertwined upon your chest and say, "Unto the Ages of the Ages. Amen." Pause for a moment, then lower your arms to your side and retire backwards to your seat and sit down.

This gesture is a tiny ritual in itself, and if used before and after meditation, or in a time of worrying distractions or stress, it can effectively seal you off from external influences. However, it obviously cannot cope with distractions and other influences whose origins are within. Neither should it ever be used to escape from contact with physical reality except, perhaps, for a brief rest. It should be practiced until the words and movements are smooth and certain. When this is properly achieved, the inner aspects of the rite can be added, as follows:

Before making the first gesture, imagine a great white-hot sun above your head; conceive it to be your spirit. When your hand is raised to your brow, imagine a line of intense light descending from the sun to your forehead. With the second movement, carry it down to your solar plexus whence it flows down into the earth. When touching your right shoulder, imagine that a horizontal component of that force exists and enters your shoulder from right-infinity. Carry the line of force across to your left shoulder with the appropriate words and thence to left–infinity. Try to be so confident in your physical actions and words that you can be aware of the inner, imaginative side of the rite. Practice often.

A Simple Ritual

To end this chapter, we will perform a very simple ritual using many of the basic techniques detailed earlier. It is a sealing ritual. Like the qabalistic cross, which it includes, it prepares a clear space for working; but in this case the prepared area is not limited to the aura of one individual but can be as large as required.

It is a useful practice to seal the place of meditation night and morning, or at least once a day, using this little ceremony. Quite apart from its avowed function, or its value as a training exercise, this simple rite—even though performed with homely "props"—can certainly help to align the vehicles and increase livingness. Success depends in part on technical efficiency, but largely upon clear intention and a driving urge to *move*.

If one room is habitually used for meditation, it may be possible to rearrange the furniture to get more room. If not, then the best must be made of whatever space is available. Resourcefulness and ingenuity are valuable magical attributes.

Before the ceremony can be performed on a regular basis, it is necessary to assemble all your physical symbols. There are few of these. Ordinary pieces of furniture—such as chairs—can be used and then resume their normal duties in the household when the rite is done for the day. Only one special symbol is required and must be used for no other purpose, and that is the ritual lamp. Up to now, a stump of candle in a saucer has been quite adequate, but seeing that this rite is to be performed on a daily basis, it is worth taking a little more trouble. A night light makes a good substitute for a sanctuary lamp, and if you can put it in a colored glass bowl or tumbler, so much the better. The color must be justified in the symbolism of the ceremony. Blue could symbolize water—the "waters of the spirit"—or blue could symbolize the Robe of the Great Mother. That is a matter for personal choice. For the moment, other colors should be avoided.

The arrangements for the rite are very simple but should be thoroughly rehearsed so they can easily and quickly be established. First, try to arrange the biggest possible working area. Next, choose one point and call it the east; if it corresponds to actual east, so much the better. Now for the furniture: one chair is selected as the throne and placed at the east-point facing west; on either side of the eastern throne are the two pillars—these can be two further chairs turned sideways so that their backs face each other across the throne. The one on the southern side is the white pillar and the one on the northern side is the black pillar.

The two should be close together, almost touching the throne so that, in imagination at least, the operator is flanked by two vast pillars when sitting down. Halfway across the working space on the east-west line, position a small table or, if there is nothing else, another chair. On it will be set the lamp. Finally, mark in some way the south, west and north points of your working space so that an equal-armed cross would be formed if east were joined to west, and north to south. Before you start, the lamp should be lighted and placed convenient to the throne.

When you are ready to start, go to the west point, face east, and stand with your hands clasped before you. Dedicate yourself to the successful accomplishment of the ritual's object—the sealing of the area; do this in any way you think appropriate. Then walk clockwise to the throne in the east and sit. Breathe in the fourfold manner for a while, gaining poise and concentrating upon your own innate ability. When you are ready, rise, take the lamp, turn facing the throne (east) and elevate the lamp to the place of the rising of the spiritual sun. See the one as the symbol and mediator of the other. Still holding the lamp aloft, walk clockwise via the south to the west, then forward to the small table. Slowly and with purpose, set the lamp thereon, thus affirming the rule of the solar logos in the temple. Retreat backward to the west, then clockwise via the north to your throne and be seated. Become aware of the pillars on either side of you, and feel their power and significance. When you are ready, rise, turn, face the east and perform the qabalistic cross. Afterward, with your left hand by your side, fingers extended and together, raise your right arm straight and point the first two fingers at the east; the other fingers should be retained by your thumb in the palm. Pause for a moment, imagining yourself as a center of purpose and power then draw an equal-armed cross in the air with your hand. Your arm and fingers should be perfectly straight and the cross formed as follows. First, the vertical shaft from top to bottom, about three feet long, then the horizontal, from left to right and the same length. Your arm should then be brought back from the right-point of the horizontal to the center. The cross should be seen as it is formed as if of a brilliant white light. At this point, say slowly and with intention, "I seal the East." Now, holding your arm in the same extended position, walk slowly to the south and repeat the cross as before but saying, "I seal the South." Walk to the West in the same manner and repeat, saying "I seal the West." Walk to the north, repeating, but saying, "I seal the North." Finally, complete the circle to the east, thus joining together the four crosses by a circle of the same intense white light. Next, lower your arm, pause for a moment and increase your awareness of the circle of light around the area, and of the four great seals that you have set upon it. Again perform the Qabalistic Cross and take your seat in the throne. Any meditation or other work can now be performed. At the end of the session, the sealing ritual should again be performed in exactly the same manner.

Although at first the rite may seem complicated and time-consuming ("how shall I find time to meditate after all that?"), quite soon the small amount of practice needed to gain proficiency will result in a smooth, effective and quick ceremony of great worth. After the final sealing, at the end of the meditation or work period, you should turn from the east, briefly elevate the lamp to the east, with actual or mental thanks for the success of the ceremony, extinguish the lamp and leave the circle.

After the session, the furniture will have to be restored to its normal position and use, but the lamp should be wrapped up in clean cloth and put away somewhere out of the light. It is worth noting that an experienced operator can generate definite etheric stresses by this rite. For this reason it is advisable to position the furniture in the same place for each ritual session.

It should be stressed that these exercises, while forming the basic components of ritual, are not in any way themselves imbued with special power. That depends upon the operator!

Why, Whither and Whence?

WHY DID YOU read this book? What is the point of it all? Where are you going now?

The point of it all is the regeneration of yourself, your community, nation and planet; the fulfillment of the plan. And what is the Great Plan after all but the sum-total of the fulfillment of each individual's own plan? So your efforts and struggles and triumphs are all parts of the whole and supremely worthwhile.

Not only does the finding of destiny make a person happier, more useful and fulfilled, but it will bring with it a state of peace— not stagnation, but a harmonious equilibrium. And, if carried to its conclusion, it can achieve peace together with progress and civilization to this planet such as is undreamt of in our present uncivilized state. A lofty goal indeed, but a true one.

But the road from karma to destiny is booby-trapped. The concrete mind is clever and inventive in protecting the status quo. Remember always that the mind is an excellent servant, but a dangerous master whose service can lead to enslavement. The quest is never easy but it *is* exciting. The inner worlds are largely uncharted territories and contain within them delights, surprises, obstacles and the occasional terror. Your guides on the journey are more than adequate if you will but recognize and use them. And the journey is lighted by the radiance of your own spirit, which is immortal and inextinguishable, whatever others may have you believe.

Jesus said, "Ask, and you shall receive, seek and you shall find, knock and it shall be opened unto you." But *you* have to do the asking and the seeking and the knocking. You also have to take the risks, the inner risks of vulnerability, the risk of appearing a fool in front of your fellows, the risk of pain, loss and rejection. To the extent that your karma has caused these conditions, so will you react, no more and no less. But the rewards, the happiness, the peace and sheer delight of re-discovery are unimaginable and there for the taking. So never be daunted.

We have briefly discussed the system of the Qabalah and its symbolism and ritual. I hope it has proved interesting and useful. But knowledge is only of value to the extent that it can be used to make life better for all concerned.

The Qabalah is an erudite and complex system. But it is also an excellent "filing cabinet" for you to use in your daily life. However, it is valuable only to the degree that it can be *used*. The manner in which each individual employs the system is unique to that being. Remember that symbols, rituals and words are merely the outer forms which you, the essential spiritual being, *use* to harness your own forces in order to become a finer being, lead a more productive life, and contribute to the spiritual heritage of this planet.

Any enquiries about this book are welcome and should be addressed to me via the publisher.